PRAISE FOR

Delivering the Captives

"We are living in a season where we must understand the victory that we have as God's children. We are an anointed people who will do exploits. Alice Smith's new book, *Delivering the Captives*, is excellent! The Lord Jesus Christ told us to first *bind* the strongman before we attempt to plunder his house. I have not read a book more comprehensive or instructive in this area than *Delivering the Captives*. If you want to be free or are in the process of setting others free, this is a must-read for you."

—**DR. CHUCK D. PIERCE**
President, *Glory of Zion International Ministries, Inc.*
Vice President, *Global Harvest Ministries*

Books by Alice Smith

Beyond the Lie

Beyond the Veil

Delivering the Captives

Spiritual Housecleaning*

*with Eddie Smith

ALICE SMITH

DELIVERING
THE
CAPTIVES

BETHANYHOUSE
MINNEAPOLIS, MINNESOTA

Published by Bethany House Publishers
11400 Hampshire Avenue South
Bloomington, Minnesota 55438

Bethany House Publishers is a division of
Baker Publishing Group, Grand Rapids, Michigan.

Printed in the United States of America

ISBN-13: 978-0-7642-0291-9
ISBN-10: 0-7642-0291-X

In keeping with biblical principles of creation stewardship, Baker Publishing Group advocates the responsible use of our natural resources. As a member of the Green Press Initiative, our company uses recycled paper when possible. The text paper of this book is comprised of 30% post-consumer waste.

green press
INITIATIVE

Library of Congress Cataloging-in-Publication Data

Smith, Alice.
     Delivering the captives : overcoming the strongman and finding victory in Christ / Alice Smith.
         p.   cm.
     Summary: "Finding and ministering freedom from demonic influence. Biblical teaching on the reality and effects of spiritual darkness, through the lens of the author's work in counseling and deliverance. Strongholds, generational sin, curses, and covenants with sin; contains steps to identification or spirits, repentance, restitution, and renouncing personal ties to evil"—Provided by publisher.
     Includes bibliographical references and index.
     ISBN-13: 978-0-7642-0291-9 (pbk.)
     ISBN-10: 0-7642-0291-X (pbk.)
     1. Spiritual warfare. 2. Demonology. 3. Liberty—Religious aspects—Christianity.
I. Title.
     BV4509.5.S6115   2006
     235'.4—dc22   2006026444

DEDICATION

In loving memory of my mother,

Martha Louise Mackechney Day,

who passed away April 24, 2006, at the age of eighty-eight.
Mother loved to teach Sunday school and did so for many years.
Her love for Scripture (the Bible was her favorite book)
inspired me to impart that same love to others.
Mother never hesitated to volunteer at the hospital or
feed a hurting family or serve in the prayer room at church.
Sometimes we wonder how we got to where we are in life.
I know the answer for me . . . it was the spiritual heritage
I inherited from my mother's family.
What a joy divine! Thank you, Mother.
I love you, and I'll see you in just a little while.

ALICE SMITH is an internationally known conference speaker and bestselling author of many books, including *Beyond the Lie* and *Beyond the Veil*, and she coauthored *Spiritual Housecleaning* with her husband, Eddie. She is a regular contributor to magazines, including *Charisma*, *Spirit-Led Woman*, and *Pray!* and makes guest appearances on the *700 Club* and *This Is Your Day*. Alice and Eddie founded the U.S. Prayer Center in 1990. They have four grown children and make their home in Houston, Texas.

CONTENTS

"She's *ours!*" he screamed. "We've had her for a long time, get away
now! Leave us alone." The spirits, furious at being uncovered,
growled from inside. With calm authority, I continued the ministry
of deliverance until she was set free. Yes, this really happens in the
twenty-first century, and not just in jungle villages on the foreign
mission field. Deliverance from demonic spirits is a significant New
Testament ministry practiced by Jesus and His disciples. Yet it is
almost entirely missing in the church today. Many Christians either
ignore it or try to reason away the need for it.

Following the 2005 Hurricane Katrina, there was ongoing turmoil
concerning the failure of the Louisiana levees. Those who lived near
them believed they were secure, but many lost their property, and
some lost their lives, when the levees did not withstand the violent
storm. Built to protect, the levees failed under pressure. We would
do well to examine our own foundations before the storms of life hit.
While they may hold in calm weather, severe storms will test them.
Our failure to fortify them with the principles of God's Word will
allow dangerous faults to form.

Some question the significance of the "sins of the fathers" and the
effect they have (or don't have) on succeeding generations. There's
not a family on earth that doesn't have "junk" in its lineage, and,
except for God's grace, we are just as likely to have brought darkness
into our families as any of our predecessors. There are only two kingdoms, and we will live for one or the other. Whatever God hasn't
planted must be uprooted, which will require our renouncing evil
connections that would otherwise limit our liberty in Christ.

It's not uncommon today to find a Hindu temple, an Islamic
mosque, or a Buddhist shrine in almost any American neighborhood.

These structures and the heathen worship of false gods that occurs within them are "welcome signs" to demons. The evil covenants established by them are defiling "the land of the free and the home of the brave." Moving from "one nation under God" toward "one nation under gods," we are increasingly more vulnerable to curses, yokes, and false covenants. Many Christian families unknowingly invite curses upon themselves through pacts they are making with the enemy.

A stronghold is an impregnable military settlement or fortress established as a base from which to stage battle. In times of war, armies built them for protection, for storing supplies and ammunition, and for planning military operations. There are also spiritual strongholds in our lives. Godly strongholds are built on truth, and ungodly strongholds are built on lies. Ungodly strongholds in our minds, wills, and emotions provide protection for the enemy and a staging area from which he can wage war against us.

How does a demon build his stronghold? He doesn't. We do. We construct the enemy's stronghold (a mindset or house of thoughts contrary to God's Word) by believing and doing sinful things. The building blocks of a stronghold are generational iniquity, traumatic experiences, and personal sins; the mortar that holds them together is the lies we believe. Demonic spirits can serve as the "foremen," directing and provoking us, but *we build their strongholds for them*. Once completed to their satisfaction, demonic spirits contend for the strongholds we've built. Those who prevail move in, become the strongmen, and then recruit weaker spirits who will serve their purposes.

An evil spirit that has risen to the rank of "strongman" has a spiritual entourage that enables him. These are the evil spirits he has recruited, over which he exerts dominion. Never forget: Demons don't serve their masters out of love, admiration, or honor. They serve out of fear and are ruled by intimidation. The accumulated demonic spirits are the measure of the strongman's strength.

CHAPTER EIGHT: UNRAVELING THE STRONGMAN'S
"Why are you here to see us?" I asked Evan. He explained that not
long after receiving Christ as his Savior, he sensed something was
wrong: something lurked inside him, especially angry at his decision
for Christ. He said he was "coming unglued." The more he sought
God, the worse it got. The closer he'd get to God, the more turmoil
he experienced. No matter what he did to compensate, his demons
weren't about to give up easily. He needed outside assistance, in seven
levels, to help him gain breakthrough and freedom.

CHAPTER NINE: CLEAN BUT EMPTY!
To maintain your deliverance, ask the Lord to create an inner longing and a mental focus on the Son of God. No one can force you to
do the right things. You must take the initiative to spend time with
the Lord in prayer and Bible study, and fellowship with godly people
who will provide a mutual support system of positive reinforcement.
Make the choice to walk in freedom. Don't assume the old habits
that led you into bondage in the past are going to automatically fall
away. God sanctifies us, but He also tells us *to sanctify ourselves*. We
are invited into a joint venture with Him!

CHAPTER 1

THE REAL DEAL

The plane trip from the States to South Africa had been long and tiring. With only a few hours to rest, I would be the first speaker at the meetings to be held in a large, racially diverse Cape Town church.

When I walked into the packed auditorium, the assembly was completely caught up in worship. As I waited my turn, I bowed my head and asked the Lord to use me to touch these Christians. Later, when I gave the altar call, many came forward for personal ministry. Despite my exhaustion that night, I knew the Lord was my strength.

One pretty Polynesian girl came to the altar and stood rigid with fear. Then, as I approached her, she hissed at me, and the calm atmosphere immediately changed. Without warning, the demonized girl flung herself to the floor and shouted, "The strongmen say for you to leave!"

"We've had her for a long time, get away now! Leave us alone." The spirits, furious at being uncovered, growled from inside her.

After casting out demons for thirty-five years, I knew this wild-eyed girl was indwelt with a spirit of witchcraft. I immediately bound the strongman, and then commanded the demons attached to the strongman to leave. As they resisted, she glared at me, coughing and hissing, but the spirits knew they couldn't continue to victimize her. With calm authority, I continued the ministry of deliverance until she was set free. Finally, she peacefully relaxed on the floor. Following the intense warfare between demonic and divine power, she tenderly wept, praising God for her new freedom.

Yes, this really happens in the twenty-first century. Satan's goal is to steal God's Word from your heart, kill any desire you have to worship or obey Him, and destroy you. (See John 10:10.) Do you realize that Satan promises the best but pays with the worst; promises honor and pays with disgrace; promises pleasure and pays with pain; promises profit and pays with loss; promises life and pays with death?[1]

Deliverance from demonic spirits is a significant ministry taught in the New Testament and practiced by Jesus and His disciples. Yet it is almost entirely missing in the church today. Many Christians either ignore or reason away the need for deliverance. Nevertheless, this is a clear command from Jesus to us, the church—that where they are present, we are to *"drive out demons"* (Matthew 10:8; Mark 16:17 NIV).[2] "Deliverance ministry, therefore, involves

• breaking demonic schemes and curses,
• casting out demons, and
• releasing an individual from demonic oppression and influence."[3]

Is the ministry of deliverance for a specialized few or is it the responsibility of us all? Mark 16:17 says, "And these signs shall follow them that believe; in my name shall they cast out devils; they shall speak with new tongues." The question isn't whether this ministry is valid and necessary, but rather how do we apply it and to whom? Power ministry should be one of a true Christian's credentials, and yet sadly we have delegated deliverance to a "specialized" few. This book will equip you with the credentials to do the works of Jesus, whether for yourself or for others.

Are we to cast devils out of a lost person only? Not at all. Jesus said in that case the house will be empty and their estate will be far worse than the start. (See Matthew 12:44–45.)

Some say, "When God saves us, He draws a bloodline around us over which demons can't pass." True, there is a bloodline, but this is drawn around our spirit; a Christian's soul (mind, will, emotions) and body can still be susceptible to demonic power where any door to darkness hasn't been closed.

This is one reason we believers are not to "give place to the devil" (Ephesians 4:27) Though we belong to God, if we refuse or fail to take responsibility for—and authority over—our lives, Satan will still have an entry point to attack and torment us. Our churches are filled with tormented people who are saved, yet not free. They are living lives as victims rather than overcomers. Chris Hayward, president of Healing Stream Ministries, has a clear word about deliverance for Christians:

> *The reality is that most believers carry "extra baggage" from the past into their Christian walks. And although we have been perfected [justified] through [Christ's] work on the cross, there is still a work to be done—a process—as [we are] being sanctified (see Hebrews 10:14). This sanctification process does not go unchallenged by Satan.*
>
> *This leads to the inevitable question: Is it possible for a Christian to be demon-possessed? I believe the answer is no. But I also believe this to be the wrong question altogether.*
>
> *Instead, we should ask, Is it possible for Christians to be tempted, to be tormented and harassed by the enemy, to open themselves up to addictions and uncontrollable habits, to have a worldly mindset and be taken advantage of by the enemy, to be subject to divisions and strife within the church, to give way to pride, to suffer with fear, rejection, unforgiveness, bitterness, anger, shame, guilt, and condemnation?*
>
> *Any reasonable observer would say, Yes! So, it is really a question of degrees. To the degree that one gives oneself over to, or falls prey to, the devil's lies and deceptions, then to that degree the enemy has a foothold in his or her life (see Ephesians 4:27). Reality would declare that we in the church need deliverance.*[4]

IT MUST BE DONE

Is there anything more painful than to do something you think is biblical, with right motives, only to discover that others have completely misunderstood and misrepresented you? In reading the Gospels we see that Jesus was all too familiar with this. Sometimes He was grossly misunderstood and maligned for doing the most praiseworthy of deeds. If we're going to take part in bringing effective deliverance to those of our generation, we too will be misunderstood. Consider this, for example:

From a field, Jesus entered a synagogue. (A synagogue wasn't the temple, which was in Jerusalem. It was for the Jews a community meeting place for worship and teaching, somewhat like our Christian churches.)

Jesus had hardly sat down when the Pharisees, those religious "snakes in the grass," brought to Him a man with a crippled hand and asked if it was legal to heal on the Sabbath. This was a trick question—they were jealous because the people followed Jesus. He had power to heal the sick, cast out demons, and raise the dead. The Pharisees were intent on trapping and humiliating Him.

Never outwitted, Jesus answered with a question of His own: "Suppose one of you has a lamb that falls into a gorge on the Sabbath. Would you sit idly by and let it die in that crevasse, or would you pull it out? You know good and well that you'd pull it out. Shouldn't your concern for people be greater than your concern for an animal?"

Then Jesus turned to the man and commanded, "Hold out your crippled hand." When the man did, his hand was instantly healed. Embarrassed and fuming, the Pharisees stomped out, mumbling under their breath about technicalities and revenge.

Jesus, knowing their intentions, moved on down the road, healing the sick among the crowd that followed Him. He cautioned the people not to advertise what He was doing, but to keep it quiet, quoting to them the Father's words about Him in Isaiah 42:1–4:

Here is my servant, whom I uphold,
my chosen one in whom I delight;
I will put my Spirit on him
and he will bring justice to the nations.

He will not shout or cry out,
or raise his voice in the streets.

A bruised reed he will not break,
and a smoldering wick he will not snuff out.

In faithfulness he will bring forth justice;

he will not falter or be discouraged
till he establishes justice on earth.
In his law the islands will put their hope. (NIV)

The persistent Pharisees then brought to Jesus a terribly demonized man who could neither see nor hear. When Jesus cast the spirit of infirmity out of him, immediately the man could both hear and see.

The townspeople were blown away by Jesus' power to deliver and heal. They exclaimed, "This must be the Son of David, the Messiah!" (See Isaiah 35:5.) But the suspicious, cynical religious leaders said, "Messiah? Hardly. That was more likely a magician's trick, or worse, it could be the work of the devil."

Jesus answered, "Whether it's a family, city, or a kingdom, if it's divided, it's going to fall. And if I'm casting out demons with demonic power, doesn't it stand to reason that the devil, then, would be working against himself, and that his house would fall?

"And, by the way, do you judge your own exorcists the way you're judging me? One thing is for sure: If I'm exercising God's power in casting out demons and healing people, then God's kingdom has come to them.

"Let me explain the procedure. The only way to rob a strongman is to enter his house and tie him up. Then you can steal his stuff."

After He chastised them for their insolence and warned them about their attitude, He said, "When an evil spirit is expelled from a person, it roves around, like a desert wanderer looking for shade, in search of another person to inhabit. Finding none, it says, 'I'll return to my previous home—my old comfortable stronghold.' When it returns and finds the person's life clean and empty, it moves back in with seven demons more evil than itself. A new stronghold is established, and the person's end is worse than his beginning" (Matthew 12:1–29, 43–45, paraphrased).

OVERCOMING THE ENEMY

In Matthew 12, Jesus reveals keys to overcome any strongholds in our lives. He describes a demonized person's inner condition as a house (an analogy) in which a *strongman* lives, along with lesser demons who serve his purpose.

"Strongman" refers to an evil spirit—like a master demon. We call his dwelling a *stronghold,* which we'll discuss later in depth. Apparently the ruling spirit, called a *strongman,* can live within the demonized person until God's servant comes in God's power and overthrows the stronghold.

Some suggest that the way to deal with such a spirit is to *cast it out* with the Holy Spirit's power. Others say that it should be *crowded out* by the Holy Spirit's presence. However, this isn't an either/or issue. While we often cast out demons, sometimes a demonized person is born again, falls in love with Christ, wholeheartedly pursues Him; *then* as he or she learns and lives God's Word, the demons become absolutely miserable and are crowded out by the Holy Spirit's presence.

One night while ministering to such a woman, we challenged the evil spirit inside her. It said (through her voice), "I hate it here (the church)! All I hear around here is 'love, love, love.'" The demon was going crazy in the presence of God's loving people. It was ready to leave, and it did.

On another occasion my husband, Eddie, was speaking to the demon in a man who, until he was saved two years earlier, had lived a promiscuous life. When Eddie said, "Spirit of perversion, it's all over," in frustration the spirit cried, "It's been *all over* for two years. I just want to know how to get out of here!" Eddie smiled and replied, "Then this is your lucky day. Get out now!" and immediately the spirit left. The more passionately a person pursues the Lord, the more anguished demons become. Being around a Christian who is seeking God is no longer any fun for them.

When a person draws near to God, God draws nearer to them (see James 4:8). When this happens, the evil spirits in the person run, just as they did from King Saul when David played his harp. (See 1 Samuel 16:23.) An evil spirit can literally be crowded out. The casting out of demons is a *power encounter*; the crowding out of demons is a *truth encounter*.

So is it cast out or crowded out? Is it a power encounter or a truth encounter? Frankly, it's usually a combination. There is a place for a believer—a spiritually anointed vessel—to exercise authority over demons and cast them out, and *you* have this authority (power) to procure your own victory if necessary. At the same time, it's almost always true that a demonized person won't be completely liberated until and unless he or she passionately pursues Christ and experiences a truth encounter.

In *Delivering the Captives*, I will show you how strongholds are built and how to identify them. You will learn how to determine the "entry point" a strongman uses to begin building his stronghold, which is key to dismantling it. The steps you'll take will provide an invaluable tool for implementing your own release and for use in ministering deliverance to others.

I will provide a list of the strongmen identified in Scripture, as well as a strategy to spoil their networks. When the strongman's "house is spoiled" and his underlings are evicted, he is effectively homeless and broke; his resources are sapped, and he's easy prey.

Many books have been written about achieving personal freedom in Christ. Each author provides a perspective on how to appropriate the work of the cross. I'll offer you what I have learned through more than three decades of deliverance ministry as well. I pray that as you read my book, God will reveal something significant to you about the tools necessary to see yourself and others set free.

CHAPTER 2

LOOKING AT THE FOUNDATIONS

Several years ago a small company was formed in New York City for the purpose of building beautiful apartment houses in an undeveloped sector. Consulting a prominent attorney, they were assured that the title to the land was clear and that they could proceed. Soon twelve houses were being built, admired by every passer-by. The workmen toiled with energy and enthusiasm, day after day, and soon the homes would be ready for sale. But suddenly one morning a message came: "Be cautious about selling those houses. You don't have a clear title to any of the foundations."

The builders were shocked. They knew this meant ruin for everyone concerned. Sure enough, each of the houses sold at auction for a meager amount compared to the materials and labor involved. Many families faced financial ruin.[1]

As a real estate agent I learned that a fundamental component to closing any property sale is having clear title to the land. This means being certain that a contracting company, the IRS, or any previous owners do not have a lien on it. (A lien is a debt attached to a property that must be satisfied before it can be legally transferred to a new owner.) A lien would block the sale until the debt is paid.

Consider the following liens.

1. Because we were born in a fallen state, Satan claims ownership to our lives; this lien is cancelled instantly when we are born again (see 2 Corinthians 5:17, 21).
2. Sin demands eternal punishment (Romans 3:23; 6:23); this lien also is cancelled the moment we're saved.
3. Sin claims power over us (in addictions and sinful habits). This lien is cancelled progressively as we build and maintain a clean spiritual foundation in our lives. We are to resist evil and draw near to God in order to be transformed into the likeness of Christ (Romans 8:29–30; James 4:8).
4. Sin, Satan, and our flesh have potential liens on our lives by the sins of our forefathers, through contracts we've made with darkness, and through unholy soul-ties between us and others. Canceling these liens is our responsibility (Romans 13:13–14; Ephesians 5:8; Galatians 5:1).

BASIC BEDROCK OR SANDY SUPPORT?

What about our spiritual foundations? A *foundation* is the base or support on which something sits. Your life, your marriage, your family, your ministry, your business, your church, or your nation, all have foundations critical to their health. Godly foundations are established and maintained when they are built with the Word of God. Jesus said,

> *Therefore whosoever heareth these sayings of mine, and doeth them,*
> *I will liken him unto a wise man, which built his house upon a rock:*
> *And the rain descended, and the floods came, and the winds blew,*
> *and beat upon that house; and it fell not: for it was founded upon a*
> *rock. (Matthew 7:24–25)*

A structure built on the Rock (Jesus) will stand. Anything we build on a sandy foundation will fall. Our beliefs determine our actions. Our actions determine the measure of our spiritual health. Paul said it this way: "We are God's fellow workers; you are God's field, God's building" (1 Corinthians 3:9 NIV).

Following Hurricane Katrina, in 2005, there was ongoing turmoil concerning the failed foundations of the Louisiana levees. Those nearby had believed they were secure, but many lost their property, and some lost their lives—the levees couldn't withstand the storm. The levees, which were built to keep people safe from disaster, failed under pressure. Perhaps we should examine our own personal foundations before the storms of life hit. While the foundation may hold during mild weather, the severe storms that inevitably come will eventually test them.

Our failure to check, review, and adhere to the principles of God's Word will develop cracks in our spiritual foundations. Defects come, for example, from unforgiveness, open doors to sin, careless living, violations of our bodies, and wrong beliefs leading to wrong choices. Jesus also said,

Every one that heareth these sayings of mine, and doeth them not, shall be likened unto a foolish man, which built his house upon the sand. (Matthew 7:26)

And neglecting our spiritual foundations will lead to collapse. Some individuals and institutions not built on the Word of God are still standing. But will they stand when the shaking comes?

The rain descended, and floods came, and the winds blew, and beat on that house; and it fell: and great was the fall of it. (v. 27)

The foundation of a structure, like the root of a plant, is usually underground, unseen. It is the core, the support, the original source. If a root system receives the right amount of water and nutrition, it will extend deeply and sustain everything we see above the ground. A building's "root," or foundation, is its most important part too. Impressive designs, vibrant colors, expensive adornments, and nice furnishings can't stabilize or secure the foundation on which a building sits. (See 2 Corinthians 4:18.)

Our youngest son once had an elementary school project: growing a bean plant from a seed. At first, Robert was patient, but as the days passed he wanted to know what, if anything, was happening beneath the soil. So one day he pulled the bean plant out of the ground to check. I explained that the root system couldn't develop if he did this, but his curiosity got the best of him. He'd compromised the roots and affected the plant by pulling the bean plant out of the ground several times. Before long, the leaves sagged and it died.

Without question there *are* some spiritual roots we need to pull. This chapter is about pulling up unhealthy and ungodly weeds from the roots of our lives! The plants we want to protect are the ones that grow from and are nourished by truth and righteousness. As the Lord plants a godly root system in you, nourish and cultivate it for continued growth.

A person can have any number of gifts, titles, and embellishments. For instance, he or she may have an attractive face, a persuasive speaking voice, tailored clothes, and a big ministry—but none of this will keep him/her from falling. If the foundation has cracks of pride, sexual immorality, corruption, envy, manipulation, poor stewardship, unforgiveness, slander, deception, or greed, in time the cracks will widen until he or she eventually falls.

Suppose while parking late one night, you slightly scrape the side of a Porsche. You are certain no one else is aware of what happened. The damage is minor and would be covered by insurance. Would you leave a note? I read not long ago about a fellow who really did that, except people were watching. And he took out a piece of paper and he wrote on it, "A number of people around me think I'm leaving you a note that includes my name and address, but I'm not."[2]

Recently, after buying groceries, I was exiting the parking lot onto a road slicked by daylong rains. As I edged forward to merge with the traffic, a young man in a huge, tricked-up truck would have none of it. Once he saw I intended to enter the traffic he sped up, shooting me a look of disgust and a gesture I'll leave to your imagination. Everyone was waiting for the light to change, so he had to stop too. But suddenly a white SUV came charging out of nowhere and plowed directly into his truck from behind, causing his truck to slam into the car in front of him. The crash was startling and destructive. If he'd allowed me into the traffic flow, my car would have been mashed rather than his.

I know nothing about the young man. Perhaps he was simply having a bad day. This might have been out of character for him. Or maybe the basis of his life is obscene, arrogant, and insensitive. God knows all this, and God knows too, whether what happened that day was a result of his cracked foundations.

THE EXPERIENCE OF TOTAL FREEDOM

As we understand our spiritual foundations, we have the capacity to deal with unresolved past issues. Paul says, in 2 Corinthians 5:17, that "if anyone is in Christ, he is a new creation; old things have passed away; behold, all things have become new" (NKJV). The moment we are born again we are *justified,* and our eternal destiny is fixed. *Spiritually,* old things have "passed away" because Jesus paid the price of sin on the cross. Does this mean everything in our lives is fixed? What about *experientially*—in terms of things passing away as we are daily *sanctified?*

Every person has three components: spirit, soul (mind, will, emotions), and body. The spirit of an unregenerate person is dead. When the Holy Spirit quickens our spirit as we believe, repent, and receive the gospel, we are spiritually transformed. This transformation includes a revelation of our sin-guilt and our hopelessness apart from Christ's saving grace. In that moment we *are* transferred from the kingdom of darkness into the kingdom of light. However, our height, skin color, clothes, house address, bank account, or marital status has not changed. The spiritual changed, the physical didn't. Once we are saved, it is our responsibility to discipline our bodies and souls to bring them into line with God's truth as revealed in His Word.

> *I beseech you therefore, brethren, by the mercies of God, that you* present your bodies a living sacrifice, *holy, acceptable to God, which is your reasonable service. (Romans 12:1 NKJV)*
>
> Do not let sin reign in your mortal body, *that you should obey it in its lusts. (Romans 6:12 NKJV)*
>
> I discipline my body and bring it into subjection. *(1 Corinthians 9:27 NKJV)*

Your soul, affected by your fallen nature, is subject to sin and to the world's temptations. Because of this, "let us purify ourselves from everything that contaminates body and spirit, perfecting holiness out of reverence for God" (2 Corinthians 7:1 NIV). For the Christian, as a new creature, this isn't about whether or not eternal life with God is a certainty. (It is.) It's about our duty to deal with our "old man," or our sin nature. Sadly, this doesn't happen overnight but incrementally, as we daily die to self. We begin to gradually see our foundation reflect the likeness of Christ.

Receiving salvation is the easy part. The ongoing call to "work out [our] salvation with fear and trembling" is the challenge (Philippians 2:12). The Greek word translated as *work out* means "to work fully until finished," and the term translated as *salvation* can also be rendered "deliverance." We are to pursue our complete deliverance from any fault that has defiled our foundation and prevented us from experiencing complete victory.

If you had unpaid bills before you were saved, your bills still need to be paid. If you had liens on your property before you were saved, you still need to clear them. When a person is born again, he receives everlasting life. But if he's to live a life of freedom to the glory of God, he will have to "work out" his salvation, that is, sanctify (purify) his body and soul.

Although it happens for some, the experience of the new birth doesn't automatically change external issues like economic conditions, family curses, generational iniquity, and unholy soul-ties from relationships, covenants, and partnerships. As we welcome the honest appraisal of when, where, and how sin took root and discover where the cracks in our foundations occurred, we can clearly diagnose where these issues came from. With the proper knowledge and revelation from God, we can clean the slate of our spiritual foundation making way for a life of victory. "But through knowledge shall the righteous be delivered" (Proverbs 11:9 ASV).

Why so much about foundations? Because structural integrity is critical to a life of victory. Satan will take advantage of a believer who leaves doors open through sin (Ecclesiastes 10:8) or refuses to resist the devil in prayer (Ephesians 6:12). So does this mean that the scriptural promises are false?

Absolutely not! It means that we haven't understood and applied key scriptural issues for our freedom. Scriptural promises are built on scriptural premises. We must learn the premise as well as the promise. We must consider the context as well as the text.

"Christ redeemed us from the curse of the law by becoming a curse for us—for it is written, Cursed is every one who is hanged on a tree" (Galatians 3:13 ESV). Here Paul speaks of one specific curse, "the curse of the law," which is broken off of us at the very moment we're saved. Yet there are other curses, which I'll discuss in chapter 4. These need to be broken as the Spirit reveals them to us. With Christ alive in us, we have the authority to do so. This is part of "working out" our own salvation, our progressive sanctification as we are conformed into Christ's image. *Spiritual warfare is enforcing the biblical promises that we inherited at conversion.*

At salvation, our sin account is settled and our sin guilt is eradicated. Then we are qualified to identify faulty foundations that threaten our effectiveness. We must ask the Lord to reveal and heal the desolate areas of our cracked foundations and reclaim what we've lost. Don't leave an opening for evil. One Haitian pastor tells this parable that shows our need for total commitment to Christ:

> *A certain man wanted to sell his house for $2,000. A poor man wanted very badly to buy it but couldn't afford the full price. After much bargaining, the owner agreed to sell the house for half the original price with one stipulation: he would retain ownership of one small peg protruding from over the front door and anything hanging on it.*
>
> *After several years, the original owner wanted the house back, but the new owner refused to sell. So the first owner found the carcass of a dead dog and hung it from the nail he still owned. Soon the house became unlivable, and the family was forced to sell the house to the owner of the peg.*
>
> *The Haitian pastor's conclusion: "If we give the devil one small peg in our life, he'll return to hang his rotting garbage on it, making it unfit for Christ's habitation."*[3]

None of us wants rotting garbage in our lives. Does the devil have ownership of even one small peg in you? Evaluate your foundation by answering these questions.

1. What evil family issues routinely reoccur in past generations of your family (e.g., slavery, addictions, poverty, beliefs that are against Jesus [anti-Christ], infidelity, pride, corruption, violence)? List them.

2. What old bills, contracts, leases, or liens have you left unpaid? No matter what anyone tells you, you are legally responsible for your debts (Matthew 22:21). List them.

3. What are the sins with which you repeatedly struggle, the ones that seem to be uncontrollable? List them.

4. In what areas do you feel cursed; areas that hold you back?[4] List them.

5. Are you drawn to the wrong kind of people through dealings, contracts, jobs, associations, and commitments? If so, name the people and situations.

6. With which of these have you or your family ever signed contracts, made covenants, or embraced membership: Mormonism, martial arts, Islam, voodoo, heathen tribal beliefs, Hinduism, yoga, Buddhism, various branches of Freemasonry, anti-Semitism, Black Brotherhood, KKK, satanic cults (New Age, Wicca, Satanism), Scientology, Unitarianism, speaking to the dead, mind-control methods, Egyptology. List them.

7. Have you ever conducted a spiritual housecleaning? "You may not take a disgusting thing into your house, and so become cursed with its curse; but keep yourselves from it, turning from it" (Deuteronomy 7:26 BBE).[5]

Hang on to your lists and continue to read. Soon I will demonstrate how to effectively cut the old roots and stabilize your foundations.

CHAPTER 3

Glancing Back to the Past

Two families from New York State were studied carefully: The Max Jukes family and the Jonathan Edwards family. The study's remarkable discovery? Like begets like.

Max Jukes, an unbeliever, married a woman of like character who lacked principle. Among their known descendants, over 1,200 were examined. Three hundred ten became professional vagrants; 440 physically wrecked their lives through debauchery; 130 served prison sentences (seven of them for murder) for an average of 13 years. Over 100 became alcoholics; six became habitual thieves; 190 public prostitutes. Of 20 who learned a trade, 10 learned it in a state prison. Their care and training cost the state $1,500,000, and they made no measurable contribution to society.

In about the same era lived the family of Jonathan Edwards. Edwards, a man of God, married a woman of like character. Out of their family, 300 became clergymen, missionaries, and theological professors; over 100 became college professors; over 100 became attorneys, 30 of them judges; 60 of them became physicians; more than 60 authored classics; 14 became university presidents. Numerous giants of American industry also emerged from this family. Three became United States congressmen and one became a U.S. vice-president.[1]

Some question the significance of "sins of the fathers" and the effect they have (or don't have) on succeeding generations. The first biblical mention of the iniquity of fathers affecting their children and grandchildren is in the Ten Commandments, where God says, regarding idol worship,

> *You shall not bow down to them nor serve them. For I, the Lord your God, am a jealous God, visiting the iniquity of the fathers upon the children to the third and fourth generations of those who hate Me. (Exodus 20:5* NKJV*)*

Before we dismiss this specific mention of generational sin as inapplicable to us by saying "we're not idol worshipers," think about twenty-first-century idols: alcohol, money, possessions, drugs, overspending, entertainment-hungry, success-driven . . . excessive *anything*.

This command is still relevant today. The immediate argument is "But this is the Old Testament," as if to suggest that we don't consider the validity of the Old Testament any longer. Yes, it comes from the Old Testament, but, as Augustine once said, "The Old Covenant is revealed in the New, and the New Covenant is veiled in the Old."[2] The Old Testament was all the early New Testament church had, as the New Testament was not yet written. Think of it—the Scriptures that motivated and set the apostles ablaze for God were Old Testament Scriptures! Jesus read only the Old Testament and freely quoted from it when He taught.

We must never regard God's Word as if it's a buffet. "I'll try a little prophecy," "no thanks to deliverance," and "one scoop of healing, please." It's alarming how selective we can become when it comes to our "pet" beliefs!

In her beautiful novel about Maine, The Country of the Pointed Firs, *Sara Orne Jewett describes the ascent of a woman writer on the pathway leading to the home of a retired sea captain named Elijah Tilley. On the way, the woman notes a number of wooden stakes randomly scattered about the property, with no discernible order. Each is painted white and trimmed in yellow, like the captain's house.*

Curious, she asks Captain Tilley what they mean. When he first plowed the ground, he says, his plow snagged on many large rocks just beneath the surface. So he set out stakes where the rocks lay in order to avoid them in the future.

In a sense, this is what God has done with the Ten Commandments. . . . He has said, "These are the trouble spots in life. Avoid these, and you won't snag your plow." [3]

The Ten Commandments are rules that help us through the troubled spots of life so we won't snag our "plow." While it's true that some parts of the New Testament invalidate some parts of the Old Testament, nothing in the New Testament invalidates the Ten Commandments given in Exodus 20. The Lord still visits ancestral iniquity on future generations.

CONSIDER EVIL'S LONG-LASTING EFFECTS

Envious Cain killed his brother, Abel, when he realized that God accepted Abel's sacrifice and not his. God placed a curse on him and his ancestors (see Genesis 4:11–14). Later in the same chapter we read how Lamech, one of Abel's descendants, followed in his steps: "I have killed a man for wounding me, a young man for injuring me. If Cain is avenged seven times, then Lamech seventy-seven times" (vv. 23–24 NIV). The line of vengeance was still in effect.

Moses, called to lead Israel out of bondage into freedom, died without realizing his kingdom potential. Early in his life, when he saw an Egyptian beating a Hebrew, he reacted in anger and killed the Egyptian (Exodus 2:11–14). Later, specifically, God forbade him from entering the Promised Land because of direct disobedience, this time again due to anger (Numbers 20:8–12; 27:12–14). Amazingly, the man God called the meekest on earth (12:3) lost his blessing because he lost his temper!

What was the root of the anger that robbed Moses of the Promised Land? It was ancestral sin. His ancestor was Levi (Exodus 2:1), of whom God said:

Simeon and Levi are brothers;
Instruments of cruelty are in their dwelling place.

Let not my soul enter their council;
   Let not my honor be united to their assembly;
   For in their anger *they slew a man,*
   And in their self-will they hamstrung an ox.
Cursed be their anger, *for it is fierce;*
   and their wrath, for it is cruel! (Genesis 49:5–7 NKJV*)*

Jesus referred to the effects of ancestral sin with regard to the religious leaders of His day.

How terrible it will be for you, scribes and Pharisees, you hypocrites! You build tombs for the prophets and decorate the monuments of the righteous. Then you say, "If we had been living in the days of our ancestors, we would have had no part with them in shedding the blood of the prophets." Therefore, you testify against yourselves that you are descendants of those who murdered the prophets. Then finish what your ancestors started! *You snakes, you children of serpents! How can you escape being condemned to hell? That is why I am sending you prophets, wise men, and scribes. Some of them you will kill and crucify, and some of them you will whip in your synagogues and persecute from town to town. As a result,* you will be held accountable for all the righteous blood shed on earth, from the blood of the righteous Abel to the blood of Zechariah . . . *whom you murdered between the sanctuary and the altar. Truly I tell you, all these things will happen to this generation. (Matthew 23:29–36* ISV*)*

Jesus accused them of continuing in the sins of their forebears—their murderous iniquities were identical to those of their ancestors.

The *New Living Translation's* rendering is powerful:

As a result, you will become guilty of murdering all the godly people from righteous Abel to Zechariah . . . whom you murdered in the Temple between the altar and the sanctuary. I assure you, all the accumulated judgment of the centuries will break upon the heads of this very generation. (Matthew 23:35–36)

So what are we to do?

EXAMINE THE FAMILY RECORDS

It's time to review your family history. You may find connections to atheism, slavery (bondage, trading, ownership), anti-supernaturalism (naturalism or humanism), shamanism, secret societies, or other false religious beliefs. (A more comprehensive list can be found in the back of this book.) Shrewd Satan is aware that one's personal sin can carry huge future ongoing implications. If our ancestors (purposefully or, often, unknowingly) opened the doors of the devil's plans to our families, we need to know it. If anything is still in effect, removing its curse will release you and succeeding generations.

Boxing heavyweight Ernie Shavers, following his fight with Cassius Clay (Muhammad Ali), said, "He hit me so hard he woke up my ancestors in Africa!"[4] While we don't actually have *that* sort of connection to our lineage, we're connected nonetheless. Covenants beget covenants. Vows beget vows. And service begets service.

Ask—humbly and gently, but ask—family members (especially older family members) if they know anything about the practices of your ancestors. Be sure not to accuse or blame others; there's not a family on earth that doesn't have some kind of junk in its lineage, and we may be as guilty as anyone.

There are only two kingdoms, and we will live for one or the other. *Whatever God hasn't planted must be uprooted.* Part of doing this is renouncing any evil connection that can prevent our freedom in Jesus. As God instructed Jeremiah (Jeremiah 1:10), so we also are to

- root out
- pull down
- destroy
- throw down
- build
- and plant.

Stop right now and ask the Holy Spirit to reveal areas of your life that you need to root out, pull down, destroy, or throw down to experience a new level of breakthrough. If God reveals any areas to you, agree to bring them into His light, repent of them, and aloud renounce further association.

And let's not overlook the godly traits of our families past. Many of us (including me) were taught the Word of God, whether from our parents, grandparents, aunts, uncles, or other relatives. Our Christian development has been a result of a godly family. Just as we need to break free from any lingering bondage, let us be thankful for Christian ancestral influences. Right now, pray, thanking God for your godly inheritance.

Believer, no matter what your family heritage, you *have* a covenant with God—the God of redemption, restoration, and deliverance. Redemption means to buy back or release; biblically, redemption is God's ransoming us through His sacrificial Lamb, Jesus Christ. Redemption is the act by which God delivers His people from bondage. Deliverance is our breaking free from bondage for God's glory.

The children of Israel escaped annihilation by the Egyptian army at the Red Sea. The Jews were later spared annihilation when God used Esther to save them. *He is still redeeming families and cultures from Satan's hands today.* Just as Mordecai said, in effect, to Esther (see Esther 4:14), I say to you, "You were born for such a time as this." Your revelation could be the key to freedom for you and your entire family for generations to come.

A few years ago I was ministering in Singapore, when a pastor invited me to preach and conduct personal deliverance in a halfway house for men who'd recently been released from prison. They'd become Christians while incarcerated, and the church had created this housing as a mentoring station. After I spoke on individual freedom, I asked if any were tormented. Many raised their hands, but one tall, slender man with an ashen face caught my attention. Slumping in his chair, he couldn't look at me. As I walked toward him, his head began to shake violently. The Spirit revealed to me that he had a familiar spirit.

Familiar spirit (see Leviticus 20:27; 1 Samuel 28:7–8; 1 Chronicles 10:13) comes from a Hebrew word that suggests mumbling in a hollow sound, as a medium. This is also what we would call "channeling." Familiar spirits are demonic spirits of witchcraft that seek to possess a person who gives his/her will to them, and then imitates the voice of another or makes predictions, promotes doctrines, and so on. This spirit can continue operating within a family.

A person tormented by this spirit will often take on demonic facial expressions and vocalizations. When I commanded the familiar spirit to loose the Singaporean man, he leapt from his chair to the floor and began to chatter like a monkey. His face mysteriously took on primate features as he curled his arms beneath him and rolled around.

I asked if he'd been born in the year of the monkey. (In Asia, it's common to dedicate a child at birth to the symbol of the calendar year; e.g., the dragon, the ox, or the snake.) He said, "Yes, my parents dedicated me to the monkey god." I bound the strongmen of antichrist, witchcraft, and lies, along with the familiar spirit, and I commanded the lesser spirits to leave, which they did. Knowing their power was gone, I immediately demanded the strongmen to leave. Then I led the man to renounce all false covenants, break the generational contracts, and sever unholy soul-ties to the monkey god (demon). He was instantly freed.

IDENTIFICATION REPENTANCE

Jesus required moral responsibility of the Jews; we Christians should no less settle our accounts. We have been given a biblical model and mandate to cancel these offenses through what we call "identification repentance." It's the practice of repenting of sins and iniquities on behalf of our ancestors (or, in other situations, of people groups, nations, cities, etc.). The accumulated influence of evil down through the generations is part of the defiled foundation we may have to deal with to experience complete freedom in our lives.

King David understood identification repentance:

> *We have sinned with our fathers, we have committed iniquity, we have done wickedly. Our fathers understood not thy wonders in Egypt; they remembered not the multitude of thy mercies. (Psalm 106:6–7)*

Jeremiah also engaged in identification repentance:

We acknowledge, O Lord, our wickedness, and the iniquity of our fathers: for we have sinned against thee. Do not abhor us, for thy name's sake, do not disgrace the throne of thy glory: remember, break not thy covenant with us. (Jeremiah 14:20–21)

Nehemiah too understood the need for such repentance:

Let thine ear now be attentive, and thine eyes open, that thou mayest hear the prayer of thy servant, which I pray before thee now, day and night, for the children of Israel thy servants, and confess the sins of the children of Israel, which we have sinned against thee: both I and my father's house have sinned. (Nehemiah 1:6)

PERSONAL RESPONSIBILITY FOR SIN

Some Christians refuse to believe that ancestral iniquity applies to us. They maintain that one's personal sin is all that is relevant. Some stake their claim on Ezekiel 18.

What do you people mean by quoting this proverb about the land of Israel: "The fathers eat sour grapes, and the children's teeth are set on edge?" As surely as I live, declares the Sovereign Lord, you will no longer quote this proverb in Israel. (vv. 2–3 NIV)

In words from the Lord, Ezekiel is speaking about spiritual death as a consequence of sin. The point is that children won't suffer everlasting separation from God ("teeth to be set on edge") as a result of their fathers' sins; the choice of where a person spends eternity is his own. The passage underscores this in God's declaration several verses later:

Behold, all souls are mine; as the soul of the father, so also the soul of the son is mine: the soul that sinneth, it shall die. . . . The son shall not bear the iniquity of the father, neither shall the father bear the iniquity of the son. (vv. 4, 20)

This isn't about predisposition, it's about eternity. A person's decision to *delight in sin and continue in it* isn't a generational thing. It's an individual choice.

The Hebrew fathers were responsible for teaching the laws of God to their children (Deuteronomy 11:19), and not to do so carried a high price (vv. 26–28). This is as true for us as it was for them. But the *way* it's true is different. As we see in Jeremiah 31:31–34:

> *Behold, the days come, saith the Lord, that I will make* a new cove-nant *with the house of Israel, and with the house of Judah: Not accord-ing to the covenant that I made with their fathers in the day that I took them by the hand to bring them out of the land of Egypt; which my covenant they brake, although I was a husband unto them, saith the Lord.*
>
> *But this shall be the covenant that I will make with the house of Israel; after those days, saith the Lord,* I will put my law in their inward parts, and write it in their hearts; *and will be their God, and they shall be my people. And they shall teach no more every man his neighbor, and every man his brother, saying, Know the Lord: for they shall all know me, from the least of them unto the greatest of them, saith the Lord:* for I will forgive their iniquity, and I will remember their sin no more.

In the study of the Bible we have to discern truths looking at the whole, not just one portion. Jeremiah isn't contradicting himself. He's not saying that people can't suffer for the sins of their fathers; rather, he's say-ing that anyone who experiences eternal death will do so because of his own sin, not anyone else's (v. 30). In the next chapter, Jeremiah says of God, "You have mercy on thousands, and send punishment for the evil-doing of the fathers on their children after them" (32:18 BBE).

One day a little girl was playing on the grass in New York City's Cen-tral Park, when a huge St. Bernard came bounding up to her, barking furiously. She burst out crying, and nothing could pacify her. "See," said her mother, "He's stopped his barking. Why don't you stop your crying?" The little girl peered at the dog, and, still sobbing, said, "Yes, mother, but the bark is still in him."[5]

The power of the cross can silence the bark of our forefathers. There is a remedy in Christ for the ongoing influence of the iniquity of our ancestors. However, we must apply His work to our lives if we are to experience its effect. It's one thing to know Jesus personally, it's another to live a life free of the consequences of the past.

CHAPTER 4

CURSES, YOKES, AND FALSE COVENANTS

We in Western society aren't as familiar with curses, yokes, and false cove-
nants as those who live in Asia, Africa, and Latin America. One reason is
our widespread anti-supernatural bias. Another reason is that our nation is
historically rooted in biblical principles. Many nations are rooted in the
occult and the worship of demons. The faith of our fathers has in some ways
protected us from the overwhelming onslaught of satanic schemes unleashed
on less fortunate areas of the world.

But have the tables been turned? For decades a doorway to darkness has
been left ajar by America's glamorization and glorification of the devil and
his angels. Hollywood (beginning with films like The Exorcist, Rosemary's
Baby, *and* The Omen*) has magnified the works of Satan.*

Then a generation of brave young Vietnam war vets came home
wounded, depressed, addicted, and rejected. Many of them were severely
oppressed.

More recently, America's immigration door swung open wide to political
refugees. Large contingents from India, Vietnam, Cambodia, Pakistan,

Mexico, the Middle East, and elsewhere, moved into our communities. Many brought their demonic worship with them. Today it is not uncommon to find a Hindu temple, an Islamic mosque, or a Buddhist shrine in almost any American neighborhood.

These structures and the worship that occurs within them are "welcome signs" to demons. They attract and establish covenants with darkness right here among us. We have become more vulnerable to curses, yokes, and false covenants than ever before, and many families have unknowingly invited curses upon themselves through pacts with the enemy.

Curses are no respecters of persons. They are unimpressed with culture or race. They afflict the rich and the poor, the educated and the uneducated. The fact that most areas in your life may seem fine is no guarantee that you are not living under a cloak of darkness.

WHAT IS A CURSE?

Curses are mentioned eighty-one times in Scripture. To curse someone or something is to declare and/or pray for harm or injury to that person or thing. The devil's agents delight to hear such proclamations, which give them opportunity to respond with supernatural power. Ignorance of what curses are and how they operate has caused many to become ensnared.

- *A curse is an evil declaration* against a person, group, place, or thing. When God commanded Israel not to take anything from the city of Jericho, He said, "Watch yourselves in the city under holy curse. Be careful that you don't covet anything in it and take something that's cursed, endangering the camp of Israel with the curse and making trouble for everyone" (Joshua 6:18 THE MESSAGE). One chapter later we see how the Israelites lost the battle at Ai, because Achan had taken defiled things from Jericho, in direct disobedience to God. Achan's actions affected the entire nation. (See Joshua 7:12–13.)

- *A curse is the opposite of a blessing.* Because of Abram's obedience to leave his heathen homeland and go to a land that God showed him, his succeeding generations enjoy His favor today. "I will bless them that bless thee, and curse him that curseth thee: and in thee shall all families of the earth be blessed" (Genesis 12:3).

God has set a blessing and a curse before each of us—conditional, "if/then" promises. "*If* you will . . . *then* I will . . ."

> *Behold, I set before you this day a blessing and a curse; a blessing, if ye obey the commandments of the Lord your God, which I command you this day: and a curse, if ye will not obey the commandments of the Lord your God. (Deuteronomy 11:26–28)*

Every day, whether we know it or not, we attract curses or invite blessings. Example: There are inherent problems with illegal drugs. If you buy, sell, and/or use them, you invite the demonic curses of that industry upon yourself. (The *abuse* of legal drugs can also invite curses.) Additionally, you'll attract the curses of potential arrest, prosecution, poverty, imprisonment, and eventually death.

If, on the other hand, you choose to live under the lordship of Christ, God will speak to your heart the next step you are to take that will open the door of His favor to you (Isaiah 30:21). Blessed or cursed? The choice is yours.

• *A curse is a judgment spoken against a person, place, or thing.* When Jesus cursed the barren fig tree, it withered (Matthew 21:20). Understanding the heart of man, He said to the Pharisees,

> *O generation of vipers, how can ye, being evil, speak good things? For out of the abundance of the heart the mouth speaketh. A good man out of the good treasure of the heart bringeth forth good things: and an evil man out of the evil treasure bringeth forth evil things. (Matthew 12:34–35)*

One example of how a judgment can curse actions: In the early nineties I wrote my first book, *Beyond the Veil*. I was certain the Lord had commissioned me to write on how to achieve personal intimacy with Him through prayer. Mustering the confidence to begin was a feat in and of itself; I struggled and struggled but continued. After a week or so, the words began to flow and my heart was filled with enthusiasm. I wrote the first four chapters rather quickly.

However, my excitement dissipated when, upon hearing about my efforts, a friend casually said, "Why would God ask you to write a book? Just because your friend Peter Wagner writes books doesn't mean you can!" He then added several other derogatory comments.

The judgmental pronouncement was like an arrow to my soul. Instead of pressing through, I agreed with his words, and for almost twelve months I didn't write another word. Rather than listen to God and question the man, I questioned God and myself. Nevertheless, I couldn't escape the Lord's voice as He continually nudged me to write.

A year later, I reluctantly resumed the assignment. After I finished the book, fourteen major publishers rejected the manuscript, so we published it ourselves and sold thousands of copies before a fifteenth publisher expressed their desire to publish it. Today, *Beyond the Veil* is a bestseller and has been translated into six languages.

Like Eddie often says, "Words mean things." Words of blessing can prompt us to move toward our personal destinies, while critical words can cause us to miss out on our blessing.

- *A curse can be placed on a physical object.* Things, even gifts, can have demonic power attached to them. This is why God instructed Israel on how to handle many of the things that came from heathen people. God's instruction to the Israelites was "Neither shalt thou bring an abomination [an idol] into thine house, lest thou be[come] a cursed thing like it: but thou shalt utterly detest it, and thou shalt utterly abhor it, for it is a cursed thing" (Deuteronomy 7:26). Our book *Spiritual Housecleaning* provides a biblical study of this concept.

In 1991, I accompanied my mother to Israel with a small group from her church. It was especially fun for me since I was reared in that church and had known some of these people all my life. Because our group was small, we were able to go to certain archaeological spots off-limits to larger groups. One of these places was a recently excavated ancient Canaanite city west of Jerusalem. Aside from a few others, we had it all to ourselves.

As we exited the bus I could hardly believe my eyes. Once heavily populated, the area now lay baking in ruins under the withering sun. Elegant tall stone columns lay on their sides in the dust. Elaborate carvings of sun gods, moon gods, and favored gods, newly unearthed after thousands of years, were neatly lined up along the cobblestone street. It was easy to see that this city had been steeped in idolatry.

One young couple, inexperienced in the demonic, had no idea how spirits can attach to physical items. Our tour director had warned us not to take artifacts from this historical site. Even so, Jimmy (not his real name), seeing what he felt was an overabundance of relics, slipped a very small idol into his pants pocket. Almost immediately he became violently sick. Our director, also a medical doctor, medicated him, but two days later Jimmy was so ill that the doctor considered taking him to the hospital.

While in Bethlehem's Church of the Nativity, I felt I should pray for Jimmy; Shaaron (named for Aaron, high priest of Israel) joined me. I approached Jimmy as he sat slumped in a chair, visibly miserable. I asked if I could pray for him and, with a sigh, he consented. I felt awkward doing this in such an open location, but I gritted my teeth, determined that I wasn't going to disobey God, regardless of my surroundings.

I placed my hand on his forehead and softly but sternly said, "I rebuke you, spirit of infirmity, and everything attached to you, and I command you to leave this man now! I speak healing in the name of Jesus Christ, the Messiah." My words seemed to echo idly off the walls of a fifteen-hundred-year-old building designed for perfect acoustics. The only physical manifestation in Jimmy was a noticeable shiver.

Not wanting to draw any more attention, Shaaron and I quietly walked outside to join our group, already boarding the bus. Within a few minutes, Jimmy and his wife came rushing out in tears. He grabbed me in his arms and cried, "I'm healed, I'm healed!" Everyone, including our Jewish tour guide, gasped in amazement.

Once aboard the bus, Jimmy, feeling the need to apologize to the group for his tearful outburst, testified that he'd never before had such an experience. He explained that as Shaaron and I rebuked the demonic presence, he experienced a burning in his stomach that rushed upward into his chest, then into his head and out the top of his head. He said he looked up at us to see if this "moving fire" that had left his body had affected us. Our conservative friends on the tour sat quietly, not sure what to do or say. I broke the tension by reminding everyone that God is a God of miracles. The group gladly joined in with agreement.

Later that day I visited Jimmy and his wife in their hotel room. When I asked if the Lord had revealed the source of the sickness, Jimmy said yes, it had been the small idol he'd placed in his pocket. After his deliverance in Bethlehem, he crushed the clay object under his feet. I prayed with both of them and advised Jimmy to repent of what he'd done and to break any lingering attachment it might have on his life. A curse had been placed on him through this forbidden object, and he knew it. I occasionally see him, and he reports he's not had a problem since.

WHAT IS A YOKE?

The dictionary defines a yoke as an arched device laid on the neck of a defeated person, to keep a person in servitude and bondage.[1] In essence, *a yoke refers to the effects of a curse.* Once the curse is spoken or released against someone or something, the yoke keeps them bound by that pronouncement. The first mention of the word *yoke* in Scripture is with regard to the conflict between Isaac and Esau.

> *Isaac his father answered and said unto him, Behold, thy dwelling shall be the fatness of the earth, and of the dew of heaven from above; and by thy sword shalt thou live, and shalt serve thy brother; and it shall come to pass when thou shalt have the dominion, that thou shalt break his yoke from off thy neck. (Genesis 27:39–40)*

The *Amplified* paraphrase says,

> *[The time shall come] when you will grow restless and break loose, and you shall tear his yoke from off your neck. (v. 40)*

It was only when Esau got fed up and took control of his life that the yoke on him was broken.

A yoke is also the wooden frame that connects the necks of two oxen to enable them to work together. Symbolically we could say that one side of the wooden frame that binds the animals is the yoke; the other side is the curse. Together they create and maintain bondage. In 2 Corinthians 6:14, God warns us not to become yoked together with unbelievers. A marriage that doesn't carry the same weight (same vision, desire, or love for God) can be a burden, as unequally yoked.

Yokes can impose pain, inflict abuse, and cause shame. A yoke can cause its wearer to feel trapped, defeated, and useless; he or she loses liberty and instead has sadness, fear, hopelessness, and tentativeness. God intends that we learn how to take dominion over ourselves, break the yoke of slavery, and then voluntarily submit to wearing Christ's yoke, which brings rest and fulfillment. Bondage to satanic forces brings only misery and devastation.

A missionary to an African nation, translating Scripture into the language of a particular tribe, came to the word *redemption* and discovered that they had no word that conveyed its meaning. When he called in a village elder and asked how to convey "redemption," the old man smiled and replied, "He took my neck out."

The missionary inquired further, and the elder explained that when Western slave traders came to buy slaves, they would place their necks in stocks attached to a long chain, then march them single file to the slave ship. If a person saw a friend or family member in stocks, and if he could afford to do so, he could pay the slave trader the price of the captured slave. The trader would take his neck out of the yoke and release him from his bondage.[2]

When Christ redeemed us, He set us free from the yoke of darkness: He took our necks out! But He also encourages us to be voluntarily yoked with Him (Matthew 11:29):

Take my yoke upon you . . . and you will find rest. (NIV)

This rest is from the drudgery of bondage to evil, from the drive to sin, and from the need to perform. Christ, who crowns our heads, also has a yoke for our necks, and He waits, patiently and longingly, for us to embrace it ourselves.

To those who are weary and heavy-laden, a yoke to wear looks like adding affliction to the afflicted. But it is just the opposite. The yoke of sin is wearing. Christ's yoke is easy. When we are yoked together with Christ, we are beneficiaries of His divine power. His strength to pull the load is much greater than our own. It's to be engaged with what He's doing (see John 5:19). When we share His yoke, we benefit from His supernatural power.

Now comes the most significant part of our lesson. Jesus said, "My yoke is easy and my burden is light; you need not be afraid of it" (Matthew 11:30 paraphrase).

A yoked ox is an ox that's ready to pull its load. The Lord wants us to be yoked *with Him*. The yoke of the world is heavy with curses, slavery, addictions, and deception. His yoke is "lined with love." Christ's commands are reasonable, profitable, and summed up in one word: *love*.

The "thou shalt nots" are boundaries set not to keep us from joy and peace and fulfillment, but to protect us from the destruction that follows wrong choices. Though there is pleasure in sin for a season, the end is death (Hebrews 11:25; Romans 6:23). Learning to wear the yoke of Christ may be challenging at first, but the love of God and the hope of heaven lighten the load.

UNDERSTANDING CURSES

Christ hath redeemed us from the curse of the law, being made a curse for us: for it is written, Cursed is every one that hangeth on a tree. (Galatians 3:13)

This verse does not say that Christ has redeemed us from every curse. He has redeemed us from the curse of the law, from having to perfectly fulfill it in order to please God and to be in right standing with Him.

Positionally speaking, every true believer should be free from every curse by Christ's redemption. Freedom is our legal position. However, not all believers have come to the point of being *experientially* free from every curse in their lives—past, present, and future. For example:

- If we refuse to forgive others, we run the risk of the Father releasing us to the tormentors (a curse of torment; see Matthew 18:33–35).

Ruba, an African Christian, had been treated brutally by her husband. He had abandoned her and the children, leaving them homeless. A loving family took them in while she rebuilt her life, but the hatred in Ruba's heart was noticeable on her face. She couldn't sleep, eat, or function; she was overcome with bitterness and unforgiveness. She complained that bugs were crawling over her body.

I read to her a story Jesus told. The end of the story says,

> *In wrath his master turned him [the unforgiving man] over to the torturers (the jailers), till he should pay all that he owed. So also my heavenly Father will deal with every one of you if you do not freely forgive your brother from your heart his offenses. (vv. 34–35* AMP*)*

When Ruba forgave her husband, she was released from torment.

- If we refuse to give God His tithes and offerings, we run the risk of Satan devouring our substance.

The pastor called to inform several church members that Mrs. Johnson was in the hospital having surgery, and he asked them to prepare dinners for later in the week. When one of the ladies asked why Mrs. Johnson was in the hospital, he responded in jest, "I think she's there to have her tithe taken out."

However, this isn't funny when it's real—when a Christian is keeping for himself what should be given to God.

> *Will a man rob God? Yet ye have robbed me. But ye say, "Wherein have we robbed thee?" In tithes and offerings. Ye are* cursed with a curse: *for ye have robbed me, even this whole nation. (Malachi 3:8–9)*

- If we seek to be justified with God by keeping the law rather than through Christ's atoning sacrifice, we are under a curse (see Galatians 3).

- If we are lost, unreconciled to God in Christ, we live under a curse, both in this life and for eternity (see Ephesians 2:1–3). It's tragic that so many live in fear and confusion, desperately and futilely trying to measure up to a set of rules and regulations.

- The Pharisees, who swore by oath that they would neither eat nor drink until the apostle Paul was killed, bound themselves in a curse (see Acts 23:12–22). Here the word *curse* literally means "to bind with an oath." For you, now consider oaths, even inner vows you have made. Also think about vows or oaths of your forefathers that need to be cancelled. Don't you think it's time to take action?

Once in eastern Arkansas, Eddie and I met a tormented teenage girl. While working with her, the Lord revealed to me that she had made an oath to Satan: She'd promised that if he would help her lose weight, she would give him her soul. Shocked to learn that God had revealed her oath to me, she admitted exactly what she did. It wasn't until she repented of making the oath, renounced it, and broke "the contracts" she'd made with the powers of darkness that she could be set free. And she was set free that day.

Have you made oaths that have opened you to the influence of darkness? Consider oaths to Freemasonry, New Age, Hinduism, Islam, Scientology, Buddhism, Humanism, Jehovah's Witness, Satanism, or Wiccan worship. Were any of your relatives involved in the organizations or movements mentioned above? Or others not mentioned? If so, repent, and then aloud sever the association you or your ancestors had with these works of darkness. For further renunciation, refer to the appendices. It is our job to discover the doors we've left open to curses and close them. Otherwise they can be operational until the end of the age. The Bible's last book says,

> *[Then] there shall be no more curse: but the throne of God and of the Lamb shall be in it [the heavenly city]; and his servants shall serve him. (Revelation 22:3)*

CURSES HAVE A BEGINNING

For every effect, there is a cause.

Nothing happens without a reason.

Each thing on the earth has its origin.

Scripture says, "Curses cannot hurt you unless you deserve them. [When they can't hurt you,] they are like birds that fly by and never light" (Proverbs 26:2, GNB).

This emphasizes the fluttering and flying of a bird, and is intended to affirm that a groundless curse is aimless, nothing more than a thing hovering in the air, that it fails and does not take effect.[3]

Curses can't make their home without an entry point; words, covenants, and behaviors can be the entry points that provide places for curses to land and remain.

Self-imposed curses can affect us as a result of believing self-condemning thoughts and/or speaking self-condemning words. Rebekah, Jacob's mother, placed such a curse upon herself with regard to securing the blessing for Jacob, from his father, Isaac, when she said, "Upon me be thy curse, my son; only obey my voice, and go, get them for me" (Genesis 27:13).

Self-condemning words are able to cause us misery until we repent of them. Rebekah grieved over the hatred between her two sons and over Esau's bitterness against her and Isaac. Out of spite, Esau married heathen women (v. 46).

Community curses affect the land. When King David sought the reason for a severe famine in Israel, the Lord said, "It is on account of Saul and his blood-stained house; it is because he put the Gibeonites to death" (2 Samuel 21:1 NIV). The Gibeonites were survivors of the Amorites; God's people had sworn to spare them, but Saul's zeal to annihilate them brought a curse on Israel. David made amends with the Gibeonites; then, "after that, God answered prayer in behalf of the land" (v. 14 NIV).

Take the city in which you live: How do you speak of it? Do you constantly complain about its humidity, traffic, spiritual void, and so on? Or do you bless it, affirm its beauty, embrace its benefits, and declare God's purposes over it? In many cities that we visit, we find Christians cursing the very place they're praying for! Don't continue to annul your prayers!

Disobedience brings a curse. When we ignore the instruction God has given us in order to live as He intended, we invite cursed consequences. For instance, He directs us to be filled with the Holy Spirit:

> *The fruit of the Spirit is love, joy, peace, longsuffering, kindness, goodness, faithfulness, gentleness,* self-control. *(Galatians 5:22–23* NKJV*)*

Paul reminds us that we who belong to Christ Jesus "have *crucified the flesh with the affections and lusts*" (v. 24). Lack of control over appetite could result in high blood pressure, intestinal maladies, heart disease/attack, or stroke; just as we can suffer consequences for living in the flesh and failing to live by the Spirit, so in contrast, self-control is spiritual fruit, giving evidence that we are Spirit-filled.

As a nineteen-year-old college freshman, I thought the world revolved around me. Every month my parents gave me an allowance for food, books, and miscellaneous needs. I lived in the dorm and had my meals provided, so I honestly didn't need much. One month, though, rather than use the funds rightly, I commandeered the cash, went to a store, and bought its most expensive pattern, fabric, and buttons for a new dress. (The equivalent of a three-hundred-dollar dress today.)

That weekend, when I returned home, I arrogantly told my parents I needed more money. Confused, they asked where my just-given allowance had gone. Sarcastically I answered that I wanted clothes, so I bought clothes.

Let me bottom-line this story: at the age of nineteen, for haughty disobedience, I received my last spanking. Are you appalled? Me too, but it changed my perspective forever. Honestly, my daddy, the coach, didn't put up with any nonsense from any kid, especially his own, and for the next three weeks I did without money. The "curse" of being humiliated with discipline, plus a zero on a biology paper because I couldn't purchase the necessary supplies for the assignment, were enough to make me remember that disobedience has its consequences.

WHAT IS A COVENANT?

A covenant is a legally binding agreement (formal or informal) between two or more parties, often written and then signed or agreed upon in the presence of two or more witnesses. Because covenants can be between God and man, man and man, or man and the devil, obviously they can be constructive or destructive. And don't overlook this: Covenants can be made whether or not each party knows all the facts pertaining to the covenant.

Constructive covenants result in our living according to the principles of God's Word. Benefits include a life of righteousness, joy, peace, provision, and blessing.

Destructive covenants, made with (or including) the devil or any of his strongmen, are established by sin, iniquity, and rebellion.

Therefore hear the word of the Lord. . . .
You boast, "We have entered into a covenant with death;
with the grave we have made an agreement.
When an overwhelming scourge sweeps by,
it cannot touch us,
for we have made a lie our refuge
and falsehood our hiding place" (Isaiah 28:16 NIV*).*

Regarding a covenant of death, one young man in our church had established a covenant of death with the devil when he was only six. Shocking, yes, but always remember: The devil never plays fair. He will take whatever you give him, regardless of age.

Luke (not his real name) told us how as a little boy he wanted to go to McDonald's, but his mother would never agree. One day, while sitting in the backseat, under his breath Luke said, "Devil, I will give my life to you if you'll make my mommy go to McDonald's."

Soon, for the first time, his mother offered to take him. But he also remembered that he felt something had changed in him that day; furthermore, over time, he became violent, promiscuous, and out of control. Eddie and I helped Luke deal with the false covenant of his tormented life and set him free from the demons that had bound him.

SEEK DISCERNMENT AND UNDERSTANDING

It's time for you to ask and answer some questions.

- What covenants have I been involved with that God is convicting me about? (Name them.)
- What are the negative effects I suffer and/or my family suffers? (Spiritual, physical, mental, emotional.)
- What are the open doors (the causes for those effects) that enable the enemy to do this to me?
- Have I ever been a part of a coven, cult, or anything similar? (In the back of the book are appendices about cults, deceitful organizations, and false religions.)

With any area in which you aren't sure or don't know, pray and ask God to reveal open doors that the enemy uses to accomplish destruction. God has given us the ministry of reconciliation, and Christ came to reconcile all things to himself (2 Corinthians 5:18; Colossians 1:20).

Once you've discovered the doors left open, take spiritual authority over the situation. If you are born again, you *do* have the authority to repent for the sins that opened the door, to renounce the enemy out loud, and to break the contracts that were made in that sin. (See appendices and *Beyond the Lie.*) Then, out loud, read and renounce the contracts made with darkness.

CHAPTER 5

STRONGHOLDS DEFINED

Though walking about in flesh, we do not war according to flesh. For the weapons of our warfare are not fleshly, but mighty through God to the pulling down of strongholds, *pulling down imaginations and every high thing that exalts itself against the knowledge of God, and bringing into captivity every thought into the obedience of Christ.* (2 Corinthians 10:3–5 MKJV)

A stronghold is an impregnable military settlement or fortress established as a place from which to stage battle. Fortresses (strongholds), or their remains, can be found all over North America—Fort Niagara, Fort McHenry, Fort Worth, Fort Collins, and a myriad of others. In times of war, armies built them for protection, for storing supplies and ammunition, and for military planning.

Spiritually, there are strongholds in our lives as well. Godly *strongholds are built on truth;* ungodly *strongholds are built on lies. In us, the latter are places inside our minds, wills, and emotions that offer the enemy protection and a staging area to wage war against our intended commitment to Christ.* A stronghold is a precursor to demonization. *The enemy builds it with the full intention of moving in and taking up residence there.*

Strongholds are developed from footholds of evil. They include pride, greed, unforgiveness, lust, envy, bitterness, moral compromise, deception, and an inner need to justify bad behavior. When we aren't intentional and watchful, as James 3:5 says, "Behold, how great a matter a little fire kindleth!" What starts as a spark can become a flame and ultimately a blazing bonfire if we don't deal with it. Mark Twain once said, "The difference between a person who tells the truth and [one who] tells a lie is that the liar's gotta have a better memory." [1] *Dishonesty is hard labor.*

A stronghold is also an inner influence that distorts our mental ability to process the truth. One illustration is Body Dysmorphic Disorder (BDD): A thin girl who suffers from this malady sees herself in the mirror as fat, a beautiful girl as ugly. Their image of themselves is distorted. A lying stronghold has been established in their minds.

Isn't it fun to watch TV's *American Idol?* So many young people, convinced for any number of reasons that they have killer performance voices, have an unfortunate gulf between their perception of how they sing and how their performance sounds to others. While this disconnect doesn't mean they have a stronghold, it does show how strongholds can be formed: by a deviation from the real and actual truth.

From a spiritual consideration, the enemy forms strongholds in us with thoughts contrary to the truth. A stronghold consists of mentally embraced images, arguments, thoughts, or theories that contradict or oppose God's Word.

Any area of unusual weakness—moral, physical, mental, or spiritual—can be a stronghold. The Philistines bribed Delilah to report to them the source of Samson's strength (Judges 16:5–6); Samson's mental weakness made him subject to a stronghold.

Satan will employ any means at his disposal to learn the areas of our strengths and weaknesses. Demonic intruders will make inroads if they can find an entry point. When we continually indulge in unbridled passions, we attract forces of darkness that can expedite a quick fall. King David failed after being weakened by lust.

It came to pass in an eveningtide, that David arose from off his bed, and walked upon the roof of the king's house: and from the roof he saw a woman washing herself; and the woman was very beautiful to look upon. And David sent and inquired after the woman. And one said, Is not this Bathsheba, the daughter of Eliam, the wife of Uriah the Hittite? And David sent messengers, and took her; and she came in unto him, and he lay with her; for she was purified from her uncleanness: and she returned unto her house. And the woman conceived, and sent and told David, and said, I am with child. (2 Samuel 11:2–5)

In James 1:15 we read these sobering words: *"When lust hath conceived, it bringeth forth sin: and sin, when it is finished, bringeth forth death."* David looked, lingered, lusted, and lost. And as surely as Bathsheba became pregnant with David's child, a stronghold was conceived in his heart as well. It ultimately led to the murder of Uriah, Bathsheba's husband and David's friend.

PURPOSES OF STRONGHOLDS

Doubtless there are more, but here are eleven reasons the enemy seeks to construct strongholds in our lives.

(1) TO CREATE SPIRITUAL OBSTRUCTIONS

Left undetected and in place, strongholds will create obstacles and restrictions to our fully obeying God and reaching our kingdom destiny. This could include unusual poverty that prevents tithing and giving. It might also involve unusual hardship and abnormal distractions, like a hypochondriac mother, a drug-addicted child, or a demonized spouse that inhibits personal spiritual healing and growth.

(2) TO DESTROY OUR SOULS AND BODIES

Over time, strongholds will destroy our well-being. They can likewise cause illness and disease. In 1 Corinthians 11, for instance, Paul shows that some who took the Lord's Supper unworthily (due to sin) were left weak and sickly; some even died (see v. 30).

(3) TO HINDER OUR BECOMING CHRISTLIKE

Left unchallenged, strongholds will hinder our purification and development into Christ's likeness, which is God's will for each of us. J. Oswald Sanders recounts a story about the great American preacher Henry Ward Beecher, who was having constant trouble with the clock in his church—always either too fast or too slow. One day, in exasperation, he put a sign over it that read, "Don't blame my hands, the trouble lies deeper."[2] Troubles seated deep within us can hinder our journey with Christ.

(4) TO COMPROMISE OUR ABILITY TO FIGHT

Strongholds also are designed to reduce our ability to stand and to battle back. Occasionally when I'm trying to help a person gain personal freedom, the person will become passive. I militantly insist they assist me to break the hold. Chuck Pierce rightly says,

> *The enemy diverts our mind by forming blocks in our cognitive processes. It's like a natural gas pipeline that flows through a network of connecting lines and systems. Eventually the gas reaches a processing station where it is processed properly and then sent for commercial use. If that pipeline can be blocked at an early point, before the gas flows out through numerous smaller lines, the gas flow to an entire neighborhood can be restricted. . . . Similarly, the enemy attempts to form a block somewhere in our brain by releasing information into it, building information up so that when new information or godly revelation tries to go in, we can't process it at all.*[3]

(5) TO CONTROL US

Another reason the enemy seeks to build strongholds in our lives is his desire to control us from within. He does this by appealing to our lower nature (our own lusts, unrealistic fears, tendencies to sin). Like a puppeteer, he pulls our strings and we dance for him. This is totally unnecessary, for Christ has freed us from the power of sin (see Romans 6).

At the same time, He didn't *remove* our old (lower) nature; rather, He *added* His nature to us. He does so to teach us to allow Christ's nature to be ours. Christ's goal for us is that we become "overcomers." The first thing to overcome is ourselves! None of us can actually lean on the excuse "The devil made me do it." The devil does *not* make us do anything.

Pulling down strongholds involves wrestling with them:

> *Be strong in the Lord, and in the power of his might. Put on the whole armor of God, that ye may be able to stand against the wiles of the devil.*
>
> *For* we wrestle *not against flesh and blood, but* against principalities, against powers, against the rulers of the darkness of this world, against spiritual wickedness in high places.
>
> *Wherefore take unto you the whole armor of God, that ye may be able to withstand in the evil day, and having done all, to stand. (Ephesians 6:10–13)*

To wrestle is to contend by grappling with and striving to trip or throw down an opponent.[4] Can you see it? The apostle suggests that we are to aggressively contend with and pull down the enemy's strongholds. If necessary, we are to violently wrestle them to the ground. The beginning of the passage commands us to be strong in the Lord and the power of His might. Only in the Lord's spiritual strength and the whole armor of God can we deal with personal strongholds and gain the victory. General (and later president) Dwight D. Eisenhower once said, "There are no victories at discount prices." He's right: Jesus bought us at full price!

(6) TO CONFUSE OUR PURPOSE

The enemy works to establish strongholds in our lives to make and keep us confused and double-minded. In that condition we find ourselves shadow-boxing—fighting the air. James 1:8 says, "A double-minded man is unstable in all his ways"—confused in his opinion and his purpose, inconsistent in everything. If you don't know God's destination for you, how will you be able to lead others on the right path? No one will want what you have.

In 1973, we were the invited evangelist singers at a church in Houston. We'd been with the pastor all week but hadn't yet met his wife. When she came to lunch with us one day, we were talking about spiritual gifts, when her husband proudly told us she had a remarkable gift. When Eddie further inquired, he said, "My wife can read tea leaves and tarot cards, and she has incredible clairvoyant gifts to know when someone is walking up the driveway to our door." He then continued to list such abilities, and when we carefully tried to explain that his wife was operating in witchcraft, and not godly spiritual gifts, they disagreed. What a sad situation for this church.

(7) TO CAUSE THE ABSENCE OF SUPERNATURAL INTERVENTION

Under Joshua's leadership the children of Israel lost God's divine assistance in their battle against Ai because there was a stronghold of greed as expressed in the sin of Achan (Joshua 7). God gave Joshua clear instructions to solve the problem: Identify it and repent for it, then dismantle and destroy the stronghold so as to restore God's supernatural involvement.

When we ignore enemy strongholds in our lives, we give place to the devil (see Ephesians 4:27) and cannot experience God's miracle power. Jesus said, "Every kingdom divided against itself is brought to desolation" (Matthew 12:25). Others will see the mixture in our lives that disqualifies us for God's work, such as an oil-and-water mixture.

(8) TO BRING ABOUT SPIRITUAL INSENSITIVITY

Seduction by a stronghold deadens spiritual knowledge, skews spiritual perception, distorts spiritual understanding, and dulls spiritual discernment. Jesus said of those who refused to see and hear, "By hearing ye shall hear, and shall not understand; and seeing ye shall see, and shall not perceive" (Matthew 13:14). Some people who have suffered this describe it as though they were hearing a sermon underwater, or as though their ears plug up, then open, then plug up again.

(9) TO ENCOURAGE SELF-ABUSE

Including masochism (any pleasure in being abused or dominated),[5] self-condemnation, and such self-destructive tendencies as abusing drugs (legal and illegal), cutting (intentionally cutting into one's own flesh), scarification (artistic cutting in patterns to produce scars), eating disorders (obesity, bulimia, anorexia), abusing alcohol or nicotine, excessive body piercing or tattooing. I'm not trying to be legalistic, but realistic. Often troubled people will cut, abuse, pierce, or cause some form of pain to themselves as a mask for the serious inner pain they feel. Many have told me they "feel" self-affliction releases their emotional turmoil.

More than three decades ago, Eddie and I led a man through deliverance who'd been recently released from nineteen years in the penitentiary for strangling another man. After hearing us teach about the Gadarene demoniac, who Scripture says "cut himself with stones," this man said, "Sometimes I sit and carve on my chest with a broken beer bottle just to see how much I can stand. Could I be demonized?" He was. And that day God set him free.

(10) TO FOSTER ABNORMAL BEHAVIOR

For instance, constant suspicion of others, obsessive hand-washing (or similar rituals), phobias (of heights, elevators, dark, water, open places, crowds, touching, closed places, germs, etc.).

(11) TO ESTABLISH DECEPTION

Including tendencies toward false doctrine, dishonesty, legalism, pride, a know-it-all attitude, and conspiracy theories. I love the answer the little boy gave his mother when she asked him, "Honey, what is a lie?" He said, "Mother, a lie is an abomination to the Lord, but a very present help in time of need." At times it seems like it's a very present help, but it'll backfire on you and blessing will turn to cursing. You'll live to hate it.[6]

WHO CAN SUFFER?

Who is it that can be targeted for and vulnerable to strongholds of darkness? *Anyone.* We've been born on a battlefield, and we're up against Satan and his army. Twenty-nine times the New Testament tells us to watch and stay alert. We must; the devil is "seeking whom he may devour" (1 Peter 5:8).

Many years in counseling and deliverance have taught me that Christians often don't realize that satanic strongholds can be (or are) compromising their spiritual and physical health. Even as we consider our own choices, we also need to remember that some strongholds result from the sins of our forefathers. Family traits are often little more than teachings and beliefs passed on from one generation to the next.

And among Christians, new believers are not the only ones who suffer from strongholds. Paul suggests that strongholds are common to all humanity, and his expression "though *we* walk in the flesh" (2 Corinthians 10:3) suggests we will encounter and struggle against strongholds as long as we're on this earth.

The apostle's "we" deliberately includes himself; in this is a warning to demonstrate that no height of spirituality, real or supposed, will immunize us from the struggle. As humans, here and now, we must wrestle against strongholds—both the ones already in us, which we are to dismantle, and the ones the enemy continually endeavors to build.

Christ's sacrifice dealt with how our sins relate to God. Because we are forgiven and cleansed from them, past sins are no longer an issue between God and us. He has chosen to put them away. They're buried in the sea (Micah 7:19).

Nevertheless, Christ's sacrifice doesn't yet deter Satan. Until the Lord returns and finally, forever, banishes all darkness, the enemy will continue to use our sins against us . . . that is, he can and will do so *until we exercise the authority we have in Christ to close opened doors and to cancel our contracts with sin.*

Let's review: A holy stronghold is a state of mind that accepts as true something in line with the will of God as written in the Word of God (Psalm 18:2). For example, the Word says we are righteous (2 Corinthians 5:21); more than conquerors (Romans 8:37); complete in Christ (Colossians 2:8–10); a royal priesthood (1 Peter 2:9); and so much more. As we embrace God's Word and live from these truths, beachheads of godly living are established—strongholds! We become what we dwell on. Truth is revealed as truth is received.

However, an unholy stronghold is a state of mind that accepts as true something contrary to the will of God as expressed in the Word of God. When we believe lies that contradict our standing in Christ, a beachhead of lies develops.[7]

With this in mind, let's consider in the next chapter how these unholy strongholds can become demonic.

CHAPTER 6

HOW STRONGHOLDS BECOME DEMONIC

Several years ago Eddie and I attended a two-day teaching conference of a well-known evangelist. At his invitation, we were sitting in the front row of a fifteen-hundred-seat hotel ballroom, which was filled to capacity.

He was teaching on deliverance, and at the end of his final session, he invited anyone who felt a need for personal freedom to come forward. Within moments the altar was packed with Christians, some of whom were exhibiting intense demonic manifestations.

So many were waiting for help that the evangelist asked Eddie and me to come to the platform to assist with ministry. I sensed an anointing the moment we stepped onto the stage. A righteous indignation welled up inside me as I took the microphone and commanded devils to leave the crowd.

At the altar, people had been crying uncontrollably, screaming, or making wild and evil facial expressions. Now, while some continued to manifest, others were freed instantly—their freedom came without anyone touching them. (The spiritual dynamics of deliverance truly are a mystery. Much has to do with God's timing, the level of demonic bondage, and the degree to which a person is pursuing freedom.) The preacher then asked us to minister personally among the crowd.

One small young woman, Mary (not her real name), was terribly tor-

mented—so demonized that four security officers wrestled to hold her down. The spirits in her screamed, "I have had her a hundred years, and she is mine! I'm not leaving!" The strongman (witchcraft) spoke in a singular voice, as if he alone was tormenting her, but he wasn't alone; rather, he was so strong that the other two (the spirit of lies and the spirit of death) were stifled, even though still present.

We were asked to take Mary to another room for deliverance. There I asked her if she wanted to be set free. (This might sound like an odd or unnecessary question, but it's a question Jesus asked. See John 5:6.)

"Yes," she replied. "Four years ago, after I became a Christian, I discovered that I was demonized. Since then I've traveled across the U.S. looking for an anointed minister who can set me free."

"Mary," Eddie explained, "there isn't an anointed minister who can set you free." She was stunned, but he continued: "Your freedom occurred two thousand years ago, when Christ died and rose again. You have been freed. The question now is, 'When will you believe the truth?'"

Mary pondered this statement for a few minutes, struggling with the revelation God was giving her. She said, "Jesus has already paid the price for my freedom." Then, unexpectedly, she exhaled a long, long sigh of relief as the demons departed. She sat up, looked around in surprise, and said, "It's over. I'm free. Finally, I'm really free!" Tears flowed down her cheeks as she gratefully embraced us. Mary had been placing her faith in the "right minister" instead of Christ's finished work!

When Mary stepped back into the ballroom, her mother gasped at the sight of her. "Honey, what happened to you? You look totally different." The next night the evangelist interviewed Mary on stage so she could share how God had set her free from her tormentors: witchcraft, lies, and death.

Mary had hungered for the Lord and pursued her freedom. When she placed her faith in Christ, the demons left her. Hers was a truth encounter: She received a revelation of *who she is* in Christ. As mentioned in chapter 1, other deliverances may require a power encounter. In chapter 7 we'll discuss how most deliverances are achieved.

FROM TOEHOLDS TO FOOTHOLDS TO STRONGHOLDS

Mary had bought into the deception that she would always be tormented. At what point did her stronghold of witchcraft become demonic—when did evil spirits walk through the opened door? Exactly when it happens, no one knows. The mysteries of the spiritual dimension make it difficult to tell exactly when a stronghold becomes a demonic habitation. However, once we embrace and identify "comforts of choice," whether from an abusive experience, a lie we've believed about ourselves or others, or a bad habit or an addiction, a door is left open and demons can gain access.

From *Beyond the Lie:*

> An unseen world of darkness filled with spirit beings is looking for opportunity to harass and torment you (e.g., see Judges 19:25; 2 Samuel 13:1–20; John 10:10.) When victimization produces trauma, demons often attach themselves to the wounded individual to advance the diabolical cycle of events. The victim's fear, intimidation, and hopelessness are now satanically supercharged.
>
> Terms used to describe demonic activity in an individual are:

- *Demon obsession:* mental or emotional obsession caused by an evil spirit, often involving confusion, hallucination, fantasy, hearing voices in the mind, and paranoia.
- *Demon oppression:* experience of feeling pressed down (physically, mentally, and/or emotionally), characteristically yielding to depression, lethargy, chronic fatigue, and sometimes suicidal thinking.
- *Demon possession:* Although the King James Version uses the word *possession,* the original Greek word means "demonized," describing a person in whom a demon dwells. The Holy Spirit dwells in our spirit; demonic spirits dwell in a person's soul (mind, will, and emotions) and/or body.[1]

Satan the strategist capitalizes on our ignorance. This is why we must learn to recognize the deceptions he's chosen to trap us. For example, in living out our love for God, we are to love and forgive others, *"lest Satan should take advantage of us: for we are not ignorant of his devices"* (2 Corinthians 2:11 NKJV).

- The Greek word translated *advantage* means "to covetously overreach, to take advantage for the purpose to defraud and make a gain."[2] Satan knows he'll gain nothing by directly attacking God, his real enemy. Instead, he attacks God's children. He does this through deception. As we reject truth and believe lies, he gains access to both enter and work in us. God loves His kids; Satan knows that hurting the children hurts the Father. Perhaps the only way to hurt the Father more is to provoke us, His children, to hurt Him through willful sin.
- The Greek word translated *ignorant* means "not to know something due to lack of information, or to ignore something due to indifference or disinterest."[3]
- The Greek word translated *devices* means "thoughts; purposes; designs."[4] The devil wants to take advantage of the Christian's every failure to cause his or her downfall.

In Argentina in the early nineties, I was to teach on deliverance—not an easy subject to present in English, much less through translation into Spanish! Nonetheless, I confidently felt that my team of eight could assist me with deliverance if necessary. Kathy Scataglini, my translator, the fiery wife of Argentine revivalist Sergio Scataglini, was so effective and appeared so fearless, I didn't know until after the session that she'd never before cast out demons.

We met in a stiflingly hot room stuffed with spiritually hungry people. At the end of my teaching, to loose the people from witchcraft, false religions, fear, and spirits of death, I led them to corporately renounce spiritual darkness.

Afterward, they were buzzing with responses. Some were jumping up and down in celebration; others were shouting with joy; a few were screaming (the demons in them were). Before I asked my team to minister to them, one of our women whispered, "Alice, I feel you should share the plan of salvation." Agreeing immediately, Kathy and I told the people how to receive Christ. I then asked any who wanted to receive Him into their hearts to raise their hands. Fifty-seven lives were born again that day.

At this point I asked for testimonies, and a nice-looking man in street clothes shared how he had driven twelve hours to attend. He said that for more than twenty-seven years he'd repeatedly heard (in his head) the word *religion. Religion, religion, religion* had tormented him day and night. He wanted answers.

He said, passionately, "When Alice commanded religious spirits to leave us, something broke off my head and left me, and I received Christ today for the first time in my life." Applause exploded; he waved his hands for quiet, and then went on. "No, you don't understand. You see, I've been a Catholic priest for the past twenty years, and I've *known religion,* but until today I haven't *known Christ!*" Then he jumped into the air and began to dance around the room. Dozens of fellow believers joined him in the aisles, dancing and celebrating his liberty.

The day that Catholic priest settled his eternal destiny, the forces of darkness were furious—their hopes for him were severely hampered. *Demonic plans are personality-specific.* They are designed with consideration of our background, our family, our education, our strengths or weaknesses, our relationships, our habits, and so on. Evil spirits look for ways to take advantage of what we don't know—or our indifference to what we do know—to produce doubt, disbelief, and defeat.

I'm thrilled to know the Lord is shedding light on subjects that for far too long have been denied or ignored by the church. Our ignorance, resistance, and indifference have resulted in many unnecessary casualties. The following passage reveals this clearly:

> *For this cause my people are taken away as prisoners into strange*
> *countries for need of knowledge: and their rulers are wasted for need of*
> *food, and their loud-voiced feasters are dry for need of water.*
> *For this cause the underworld has made wide its throat, opening its*

mouth without limit: and her glory, and the noise of her masses, and her loud-voiced feasters, will go down into it. (Isaiah 5:13–14 BBE*)*

DOWN INTO DEATH, UP INTO LIFE

Again, while I can't say precisely how and when a stronghold becomes demonic, it typically doesn't happen overnight. It comes about through a process of sin. From my experience and the experience of others, two exceptions tend to be in areas of sexual perversion and/or witchcraft. Why? I can only guess that sexual perversion, the likes of which caused God to be so angry that He demolished the cities of Sodom and Gomorrah along with their inhabitants, is an insult to His creative purposes. (See Exodus 20:5; 1 Kings 14:22–24; 16:25–26; 2 Kings 17:7–23 NIV.) Witchcraft, which cost King Saul his life, severely insults God's sovereignty. (See Deuteronomy 18:9–12; 1 Samuel 15:23; 28:7–18; 2 Chronicles 33:6 NIV.)

Whatever the case, it's clear that experimentation with these is a fast track to demonization and demonic strongholds. And how does a demon build his stronghold? He doesn't—*we do.* That's right. We construct the enemy's stronghold (a mindset, or house of thoughts, that's contrary to God's Word) by believing and doing sinful things. A stronghold's building blocks, so to speak, are generational iniquity, traumatic experiences, and personal sins; the mortar that holds them together is what we believe and do that's contrary to God's truth.

Demonic spirits can serve as the "foremen" or bosses, directing and provoking us. But in the final analysis, *we build their strongholds for them.* Once the stronghold we've constructed is completed to their satisfaction, demonic spirits contend for it. The one who prevails moves in, becomes the strongman, then sets about to recruit similar but weaker spirits to serve his purposes. This process can be repeated (even simultaneously) with other open doors to strongholds. This is how a severely demonized person can have two, three, or more strongmen controlling a stronghold.

Here's the sequence:

1. *A thought:* One begins to think about sin . . . any sin.
2. *A feeling:* He emotionally desires to commit that sin.

3. *An act:* He willfully chooses and engages in that sin.
4. *A habit:* He continues to give way to the sin, which forms a pattern.
5. *A stronghold:* He has an inner pulling toward that sin, increasingly overpowering and uncontrollable.
6. *An empowerment:* A like-minded demonic spirit enters the stronghold the person has built and begins to express its own evil desires through him. The man's evil desires carry an evil anointing. The demon controls and keeps him bound. Until he repents of his sin, turns from and renounces it, and commands the demons to leave, he will fall progressively into deeper levels of sin. Furthermore, the evil spirit will recruit other spirits to come and help maintain the stronghold.

In a real life example, consider how young Karla Faye Tucker became one of America's most infamous murderers.

"With a pickaxe and fifty-seven blows," Karla Faye Tucker "took part in one of the most gruesome double murders in Texas state history. Her life had already started to go downhill at an early age. Surrounded by the mischievous demons out to do her in, her pretty figure wove in and out of crime when but a little girl. She was without direction, void of love, reaching out to find no guide but her own misfortune."[5]

> *Karla Faye Tucker had a difficult childhood; her father had given up on her as a child and her mother died from the effects of drug abuse on Christmas Eve 1979, when she [Karla] was twenty, ending her relationship with the only person whom, she said, had always really loved her. It is a sadly common story in murder cases—a young person gets into drugs and then into crime after a poor or disturbed childhood.*
>
> *On marijuana at age 10; heroine at 11; sex at 12; prostitution at 14; a quick marriage and divorce at 16; and double murder at 23.*[6]

"The influence of others—peer pressure," she explained to Terry Meeuwsen [co-host of *The 700 Club*]. "My sisters were into drugs, and they had a friend who was older; they always hung around with older people. There were a lot of drugs."[7]

In a 1990 interview with *LifeWay Church* magazine, she recalled the night of her crime.

> *"I saw what he [Jerry Dean] had done to Shawn [her girlfriend], and I was really mad (because) I was really protective of her,"* Karla Faye said. *"I thought,* Yeah, I'll get even with him! *My idea of getting even with him meant confronting him, standing toe to toe, fist to fist."*
>
> *As the party progressed, the bitter feelings raged; the pills added to the animosity and excitement [as] the very night itself seemed to heat up Karla Faye's anger. While most of the people at the party were enjoying the haze of their own smoky brain, Karla Faye, Danny, Shawn, and another friend, Jimmy, retreated to a corner in the kitchenette to slur their vehemence over wife-beater Dean. Their intention was revenge, but at that point the kitchen-table dialogue just spoke in generalities. Eventually sister Kari and her friend Ronnie joined the conversation, and the threats melted into sardonic laughter, eventually fading into idle, tough talk that dissipated as the last of the capsules were downed and the final inhalations of the final joints were savored.*

Later that night they stepped inside Dean's unlocked house, where Jerry Dean and Deborah Thornton, his mistress, were sleeping.

> *"Who's out there?" came Dean's all-too-familiar growl.*
>
> *Karla Faye felt herself waver; one foot aimed for the front door, the other toes dug in defiantly for a fight. Her hands clenched into fists. While she froze in this confusion, Danny had already reacted. He had grabbed a hammer from beside the toolbox and was now racing for the bedroom. Karla Faye followed instinctively. From the doorway of the room, she watched Danny's weapon strike the figure of Dean, who had half-risen from the covers. The blow, which had struck his head, jolted him backward. Karla Faye found the violence thrilling.*
>
> *The sight she saw was evil, magnetic. She wanted to partake of the sacrifice and roll in the wantonness. Danny's bludgeons continued, for he seemed to be releasing his own frustrations. There was no role for her in this ritual—until she saw the girl almost buried under the covers by the*

other side of the bed, where she had slipped and was now attempting to hide herself.

Reaching back into the living room, Karla Faye grabbed the first murderous thing she saw, a pickaxe, three feet long and easy to grip. Effortlessly she lifted it and returned to the chamber. Danny, his senses satiated for the moment, paused to watch, followed her curious movements as she circled the bed and raised the axe overhead.

The girl, later identified as Deborah Thornton, had screamed only once. Danny threw a blanket over her head, daring Karla to hit the target blindfolded.

Karla Faye Tucker busted loose.[8]

[In photos at her trial, Karla Faye Tucker] looked dour and apathetic—in a word, dead. However, at the time of her execution, [she] looked like an entirely different person: vibrant, kind, gentle, gracious, [with] a radiant smile. She had found God's gift of grace in Jesus Christ from a Bible unceremoniously left in her cell by one of the jail chaplains. . . . After fourteen years on death row, [she] was, by all accounts, a woman who had passed from death to life.[9]

Never giving up, the Father searched out her spirit; reaching down in order to lift up, He loved her into mercy and forgiveness she'd never known. The Lord redeemed her out of reach from hell's wretched depths and into heaven's glorious light. And this He has done for every one of us saved only by grace.[10]

You were dead in the trespasses and sins in which you once walked, following the course of this world, following the prince of the power of the air, the spirit that is now at work in the sons of disobedience— among whom we all once lived in the passions of our flesh, carrying out the desires of the body and the mind, and were by nature children of wrath, like the rest of mankind. But God, being rich in mercy, because of the great love with which he loved us, even when we were dead in our trespasses, made us alive together with Christ—by grace you have been saved—and raised us up with him and seated us with him in the heavenly places in Christ Jesus, so that in the coming ages he might show the immeasurable riches of his grace in kindness toward us in Christ Jesus. For by grace you have been saved through faith. And this is not your own doing; it is the gift of God, not a result of works, so that no one may boast. For we are his workmanship, created in Christ Jesus for good works, which God prepared beforehand, that we should walk in them. (Ephesians 2:1–10 ESV)

The "you's" in verse one are second person plural. This means the finger points to all of us: *We were dead in our sins.*[11] We can be freed from sin and released from strongholds only because of God's amazing grace.

Progressive traumatic events and open doors to perversion, rejection, witchcraft (drugs), and hatred developed Karla Faye Tucker's strongholds. She became a demonized young woman. Note the sequence in her life:

- Abandoned and rejected by parents
- Overarching vulnerability
- Sin
- Habits (formed to numb the pain)
- Compulsive thoughts (ongoing obsession), controlling desires
- Strongholds
- Death (this isn't always physical; sometimes psychological, mental, or emotional).

As you can see, Karla Faye Tucker's life was a textbook example of what we're learning. Strongholds are serious. We *must* grasp the significance of binding the strongmen that rule them, and then demolishing them, if we are to bring freedom to the oppressed.

Let's look now at how strongmen are bound.

CHAPTER 7

THE STRONGMAN: BINDING IS THE KEY

The story of the Philistine giant illustrates the power of a strongman. Goli-
ath was over nine feet tall and his armor weighed about one hundred
twenty-five pounds. The point of his spear alone weighed about fifteen
pounds. His warriors had gathered for battle against Israel, pitching their
camp at Ephes-dammim, which means "boundary of blood." No doubt death
was Goliath's intention—the giant and his army were there to defy and
destroy God's people. Every Hebrew fighter feared for his life.

Each day, for forty days, Goliath stood atop his hill and shouted to
Israel,

> *Why bother using your whole army? Am I not Philistine enough for*
> *you? And you're all committed to Saul, aren't you? So pick your best*
> *fighter and pit him against me. (1 Samuel 17:8* THE MESSAGE*)*

No soldier among King Saul's ranks was willing to stand up against the
giant. One day, David, the youngest of the sons of Jesse, sent to the camp with
food, heard Goliath's taunts and asked, "Who does he think he is, anyway, this
uncircumcised Philistine, taunting the armies of God-Alive?" (v. 26 THE MES-

SAGE). *David's older brothers, embarrassed by him and belittling of him, tried to intimidate David so he would leave.*

Refusing to be deterred, David went to King Saul and offered to kill Goliath, saying that even as he had struck and killed a lion and a bear, so he would do the same with the giant, for the Lord would deliver him just as He had before.

Then David took his shepherd's staff, selected five smooth stones from the brook, and put them in the pocket of his shepherd's pack, and with his sling in his hand approached Goliath.

As the Philistine paced back and forth, his shield bearer in front of him, he noticed David. He took one look down on him and sneered—a mere youngster, apple-cheeked and peach-fuzzed. The Philistine ridiculed David. "Am I a dog that you come after me with a stick?" And he cursed him by his gods. "Come on," said the Philistine. "I'll make roadkill of you for the buzzards. I'll turn you into a tasty morsel for the field mice."

David answered, "You come at me with sword and spear and battle-ax. I come at you in the name of God-of-the-Angel-Armies, the God of Israel's troops, whom you curse and mock. This very day God is handing you over to me. I'm about to kill you, cut off your head, and serve up your body and the bodies of your Philistine buddies to the crows and coyotes. The whole earth will know that there's an extraordinary God in Israel. And everyone gathered here will learn that God doesn't save by means of sword or spear. The battle belongs to God—he's handing you to us on a platter!"

That roused the Philistine, and he started toward David. David took off from the front line, running toward the Philistine. David reached into his pocket for a stone, slung it, and hit the Philistine hard in the forehead, embedding the stone deeply. The Philistine crashed, facedown in the dirt.

That's how David beat the Philistine—with a sling and a stone. He hit him and killed him. No sword for David! Then David ran up to the Philistine and stood over him, pulled the giant's sword from its sheath, and finished the job by cutting off his head. When the Philistines saw that their great champion was dead, they scattered, running for their lives. (1 Samuel 17:40–51 THE MESSAGE*)*

THE STRONGMAN'S STRENGTH, THE STRONGMAN'S WEAKNESS

Consider what Goliath can teach us about a strongman. Like the giant, a strongman is the greatest among a household of demons. The giant intimidated; a strongman intimidates. Goliath caused fear; a strongman creates fear. Goliath controlled the territory, threatening anyone who tried to take it; a strongman threatens us with lies, accusation, and fear, saying we will never be free.

David, in the strength of Almighty God, who is greater than any giant, defeated Goliath with a quick and decisive blow to the forehead. As David did, we have to go for the head (the lead strongman). Once he fell, David cut off Goliath's head with Goliath's own sword. Our sword is the "sword of the Spirit, which is the word of God" (Ephesians 6:17). We cut off the enemy's head with the authority of the Word. When Goliath's head was severed, the Philistines ran from their encampment. When a strongman has his head cut off (when his strength is bound), the demons in the stronghold will be ready to flee as well.

A strongman is the ruling demon that resides in a stronghold (a house in which lesser demons hide) and uses it for his own benefit. Jesus said, "How can one enter into a strong man's house, and spoil his goods, except he first bind the strong man? and then he will spoil his house" (Matthew 12:29). Jesus taught that a person's lasting freedom is gained through first binding the household boss (the strongman), then commanding the spirits operating under him to leave the house. This causes the strongman to lose his authority and strength; next we evict the lesser demons, and lastly we can command the strongman to vacate.

Why does Jesus tell us to bind the strongman first? In the case of a demonic stronghold, the strength of the leader (strongman) apparently is determined by the collective strength and number of lesser demons who serve him. He doesn't strengthen them—rather, they strengthen him.

Jesus tells us how to dislodge and discharge the strongman: weaken, then evict. To weaken him, we are to bind him; once he is bound (unable to act), we cast out his "servants." When the "house" (the tormented person) is empty of lesser demons, then the strongman has no remaining support system, and we throw him out.

Through helping thousands realize personal freedom, I have come to believe that God has identified the strongmen in Scripture. Knowing their identity is key to unlocking lives from demonic strongholds. (We'll soon look at these.)

THE ENCOUNTER

In the Matthew 12 story, Jesus is the anointed vessel exercising spiritual authority over evil spirits that had kept a man blind and deaf. When He commanded them to leave, they did. The Pharisees then accused Him of casting out demons in the devil's power, and Jesus responded, essentially, that "Satan wouldn't permit a weaker one to defeat him; that Satan is helpless before me proves that I am from God and am stronger than he is."

After this, Jesus gave further instruction concerning the process of a power encounter. From *The Message:*

> *How in the world do you think it's possible in broad daylight to enter the house of an awake, able-bodied man and walk off with his possessions unless you tie him up first? Tie him up, though, and you can clean him out. . . .*
>
> *When a defiling evil spirit is expelled from someone, it drifts along through the desert looking for an oasis, some unsuspecting soul it can bedevil. When it doesn't find anyone, it says, "I'll go back to my old haunt." On return it finds the person spotlessly clean, but vacant. It then runs out and rounds up seven other spirits more evil than itself and they all move in, whooping it up. That person ends up far worse off than if he'd never gotten cleaned up in the first place. (Matthew 12:29, 43–45)*

From the *English Standard Version:*

> *How can someone enter a strong man's house and plunder his goods, unless he first binds the strong man? Then indeed he may plunder his house. . . .*
>
> *When the unclean spirit has gone out of a person, it passes through waterless places seeking rest, but finds none. Then it says, "I will return to my house from which I came." And when it comes, it finds the house empty, swept, and put in order. Then it goes and brings with it seven other spirits more evil than itself, and they enter and dwell there, and the last state of that person is worse than the first.*

(1) ENTER THE STRONGMAN'S HOUSE

Jesus said that to conquer the strongman, we must enter his "house." This is because we will find the strongman and his network of demons in the stronghold. The Greek word for *house* means "a domestic household that is a familiar abode." By implication, the strongman is comfortable and familiar with the person's life and with the resident demons in the house.

(2) BIND THE STRONGMAN

Jesus says that once we "enter the house"—that is, find the stronghold—we bind the strongman. But why bind him? Why not simply cast him out?

The reason has to do with the source of the strongman's strength. Consider, for example, a desert nomad: The number of camels, goats, livestock, and servants, along with the value of his possessions, is the measure of his wealth. If he is stripped of what he possesses, he loses his wealth and his influence.

Again, a demonic spirit that has assumed the rank of "strongman" has a spiritual entourage that empowers him. This is composed of the evil spirits he has attracted to his stronghold, and over these he exerts dominion. Demons don't serve their masters out of love, admiration, or honor. They serve out of fear and are ruled by intimidation. The spirits the strongman has accumulated, the demons through whom he works, are a measure of his strength.

This is why we are to bind before casting out: initiating a fight with the strongman isn't wise. Not only is he *strong,* he also would take pleasure in a "power struggle." We would be coming against him at the peak of his might. Instead, we bind first, and then we clean his house by casting out the lesser spirits who work for him.

We have seen ministers and ministry teams trying to cast out the strongman without first binding him. Know this: A strongman is often content to sacrifice the demons under his rule in order to save himself. He'll let them be ejected from the stronghold like a bird pushing its fledglings out of the nest.

When this happens, the minister stops, believing that the person is free and that the battle is won. While the team rejoices and celebrates success, the strongman smugly sits back and plans when he'll invite the evicted demons to return. And often they *will* return. This is why uninformed and untrained teams can deal repeatedly with the same demons. If the whole job of deliverance isn't done, after a while the demons come back to resume their evil game.

(3) SPOIL THE STRONGMAN'S STRENGTH

So after entering the house, we bind the strongman—weaken the Goliath—in the name of Jesus Christ, the one who is greater than any demon. Once he's bound, we "spoil" the strength of his house (Matthew 12:29). What does this mean?

The Greek word *spoil* means "to seize asunder" or "to plunder." *Webster's*[1] says *seize* means:

- to take possession of by legal process;
- to bind or fasten together with a lashing of cord;
- to take or lay hold of forcibly;
- to capture and arrest.

The word *asunder* means:

- to move apart from each other (wide apart);
- to be torn into parts.[2]

The word *plunder* means:

- to take by force;
- to pillage, loot, steal, and sack.[3]

I believe Jesus gave us powerful and intense words to describe the authority He has given us for deliverance. For spoiling the stronghold, this is my paraphrase of what He laid out for us:

> *Run suddenly to the house, break down the door, grab hold of the boss (strongman), then bind and gag him.*
>
> *Next, grab the lesser colleagues (demons) and separate them from one another.*
>
> *Now, pillage, loot, and plunder the house. Overwhelm every demon, commanding it to get out and never return. Force them all out with a firm command.*
>
> *Once the others are gone, go to the boss (strongman) and tell him to get lost. As you do, inform him that neither he nor his friends can ever return.*
>
> *Take the keys, lock the door, and speak a blessing over the house.*

SPIRIT OF . . .

Before I continue, I want to be clear that there are many different models, techniques, ideas . . . *ways* to conduct deliverance. I don't have any argument with other styles as long as they are biblical and produce lasting freedom in the person helped. Thank God for the many ministries who take the battle to the gates of the enemy.

I believe the majority of the biblical strongmen are identified as a "spirit of _____." The Hebrew and Greek words for *spirit* (*ruach* and *pneuma*) speak of "wind," or "hard breath," of which there are two kinds.

The first kind is the Holy Spirit. This wind is unseen, but the Spirit's manifestation in a person's life *is* like a sweet, vitalizing breeze of refreshment.

The second kind is a not-of-God (demonic) spirit. This is also unseen, and when a demon manifests in a life, it produces evil; this wind breathes deception, darkness, and death.

What are the strongmen? For instance, "God hath not given us the *spirit of fear;* but of power, and of love, and of a sound mind" (2 Timothy 1:7). A spirit of fear is a strongman.

Or, "The Lord has poured into them a *spirit of dizziness;* they make Egypt stagger in all that she does" (Isaiah 19:14 NIV). A spirit of "dizziness" (unbelief or confusion) is a strongman.

Or, "Ye have not received the *spirit of bondage* again to fear; but ye have received the Spirit of adoption, whereby we cry, Abba, Father" (Romans 8:15). A spirit of bondage is a strongman.

Or, "The spirit of the Lord God . . . hath sent me . . . to appoint unto them that mourn in Zion, to give unto them beauty for ashes, the oil of joy for mourning, the garment of praise for the *spirit of heaviness;* that they might be called trees of righteousness, the planting of the Lord, that he might be glorified" (Isaiah 61:1, 3). The spirit of heaviness is a strongman.

Likewise, while for one person Jesus commanded the *spirit of infirmity* to be gone, to another He would say, "Be healed." One situation had a demon behind the infirmity, while the other didn't (e.g., see Luke 13:11–12; John 5:5–8).

THE SIGNIFICANCE OF THREES

In the back of the book find Appendix 1: "Apparent Demonic Groupings List," a tool designed to give you help in the future. As I've facilitated deliverance in various nations, languages, and cultures, I've identified and documented patterns of demonic associations. The maxim says that "birds of a feather flock together," and this is seemingly true in the kingdom of darkness. Certain demonic types tend to congregate in people's lives, and they seem to associate with the same strongmen. For example, demons of terror are often found with demons of hysteria, both serving a spirit of fear (strongman).

Over time, if a person continues to open doors of sin, the number of strongmen in his or her life tends to increase; common are sets of three strongmen with their strongholds. As I've studied this, I've learned that the number three is mentioned 485 times in the Bible. Engineers tell us that of all the geometric designs, the three-sided triangle is the strongest possible.[4]

The importance of this doesn't escape the devil's plans. Here are some key threes:

- Jonah was in the fish three days and three nights (Jonah 1:17).
- Jesus was in the grave three days (Matthew 27:63).
- There are three in the Godhead: Father, Son, and Holy Spirit (1 John 5:7).
- Moses was hid for three months (Exodus 2:2).
- Sacrifices are done three times a year (2 Chronicles 8:12–13).
- There are three that bear witness in earth: the spirit, the water, and the blood (1 John 5:8).
- Three unclean spirits like frogs coming up out of the dragon, the beast, and the false prophet (Revelation 16:13).
- There are three parts to man: spirit, soul, and body (1 Thessalonians 5:23).
- A threefold cord isn't easily broken (Ecclesiastes 4:12).

Many demonized people are bound with three "cords" of strongholds. My finding is that when there are three strongmen in a person, one will always be the strongest of the three. (Furthermore, in the devil's web of evil conduits, even when three strongmen work together to defeat a life, they'll still connect with other networks to keep a person confused and bound.)

The following sets of three are those that I've seen consistently work together. The spirits of:

- Fear, Heaviness, and Bondage
- Fear, Lies, and Heaviness
- Fear, Infirmity, and Heaviness
- Antichrist, Witchcraft, and Lies
- Perversion, Infirmity, and Death
- Unbelief, Error, and Lies
- Seducing Spirits, Perversion, and Whoredom
- Jealousy, Pride, and Lies
- Familiar Spirits, Witchcraft, and Antichrist
- Infirmity, Deaf and Dumb, and Death

- Pride, Error, and Seducing Spirits
- Unbelief, Antichrist, and Seducing Spirits
- Bondage, Perversion, and Whoredom
- Bondage, Heaviness, and Lies
- Jealousy, Witchcraft, and Antichrist
- Bondage, Death, and Infirmity

Regarding strategy, determine to operate according to what the Lord tells you to do, whether that means starting with the strongest or the weakest of the three strongholds. Additionally, remember that if the person has lived in and cooperated with darkness for a long time, there may be two or more sets of clustered strongholds (more than one "threefold cord").

As I mentioned earlier, it's not incumbent upon us to fully understand the spiritual dimension; there *are* mysteries that, unless the Lord chooses to completely reveal them to us, we will not comprehend in the here and now. Even so, how do we know *which* strongmen are present? Let's consider several situations; know that as you are thinking logically about what you see and sense, you must never neglect to ask the Lord for confirmation and for the anointing to shatter the network. (Perhaps here you'll also find the "Apparent Demonic Groupings List" helpful.)

Valerie comes to the altar for prayer, and she begins to shake. As I pray, the shaking intensifies. Now her lips are quivering, her face is sad, and her body is trembling as her shoulders fall forward. What strongman is she manifesting? *A spirit of fear.* Spirits behave as they are. Fearful spirits manifest fearful emotions.

Also, in light of how demons operate in network, the other two spirits in this cord are probably a spirit of bondage and a spirit of heaviness. The fear is the trembling, the heaviness suggests the slumped shoulders, and bondage manifests as though she is paralyzed, unable to move. No matter what you think you know, always ask the Holy Spirit to reveal the network, because the threefold strongmen could also be fear, infirmity, and heaviness (see list above). As you name the three strongmen, there will be a reaction from the person to suggest that you're on track.

Worth mentioning: the reason the three strongmen in Valerie wouldn't be fear, lies, and heaviness (see list above) is that a lying spirit always manifests differently, by an extreme shaking of the head "no," or a putting of hands over ears to keep from hearing the rebuke and dismissal.

Another example: Josh asks for prayer. When we sit down to pray, he complains that his ears are popping and he can't hear us. As we continue to ask the Lord for breakthrough, Josh opens his eyes to tell us that the devils are saying he isn't saved and never will be. This strongman? *A spirit of unbelief.* Unbelief correlates with generational iniquity; his family could have been atheist or communist or simply uncommitted.

Josh had wondered why he's always struggled with hearing sermons or memorizing the Word. Now he knows that unbelief has affected his life. With this spirit, error and lies network together. Error is indicative of one who had no background or training in spirituality; though now saved, that person has a tendency to become legalistic with wrong doctrine. The spirit of lies loves to question salvation issues and create doubt.

Angela, a teenager, comes to the office for prayer. Her heart races; she feels faint. She is tormented in the night, when she feels unseen hands touching her body. For several years Angela has been dabbling in the occult through music and games, and when her mother told her to stop, she rebelled. She tried cocaine six months ago, and now she's addicted.

But she wants help. As I ask the Lord to reveal the strongmen, a wicked, sinister expression comes across her face. Her eyebrows raise, and her eyes are wild with evil. Staring at me, she hisses. Strongman? *A spirit of witchcraft.* "Rebellion is as the sin of witchcraft" (1 Samuel 15:23); the Greek word for *witchcraft* is *pharmakeia,* which denotes drugs and sorcery. Angela's defiance and experimentation with mind-altering drugs opened the door. The tormented girl violently shakes her head as I take authority over the spirits. She taunts that God can't help her (spirit of lies). The third is a spirit of antichrist, which enhances hatred, spite, bitterness, and rebellion.

Next, we must undertake the process of unraveling and dismantling the stronghold.

CHAPTER 8

Unraveling the Strongman's Strength

EVAN'S OLD LIFE

LEVEL ONE

When Evan walked into the room, none of us doubted he needed a break-through. He was young, but the lines etched on his face suggested otherwise. Evan walked with humped shoulders that indicated someone two or three times his age.

His maternal great-grandfather had once been Worshipful Master of the Masonic lodge in his central-Mississippi hometown. Most of his relatives were proudly committed Freemasons, and anyone in the family (like Evan) who didn't follow the same path experienced isolation. Although he didn't really know or understand why, Evan felt he didn't want to get involved in Freemasonry, and yet the family's rejection had been a terrible price to pay.

Evan had also been born out of wedlock; the stigma from this had followed him throughout his life. His paternal grandfather hadn't loved him because he was "the bastard."

A higher-than-average percentage of his father's family suffered from heart problems. Several aunts, uncles, and cousins had died young; his father himself died a few years after Evan was born, though not from a heart problem.

Many of his aunts and uncles suffered paranoia. For no clear reason, one aunt had six locks installed on her front and back doors; another uncle was more than ready to kill the first intruder that came near his house. Both sides of Evan's family were a "mess."

Looking at the stronghold graphic on page 81, you can see how the sins, sicknesses, and generational evils of Evan's family (Level One) brought insight into his own issues. As it happens, the spirits of antichrist, lies, witchcraft, death, bondage, heaviness, fear, and infirmity were active in his lineage before he was even conceived.

LEVEL TWO

When Evan's mother was pregnant with him, she suffered severe trauma in an auto accident. For many nights afterward, she had nightmares about the man in the car that had sideswiped them. He had been killed instantly, and she wondered whether the image of terror on his face before impact would ever go away. Fear and trauma were present and pervasive before Evan's birth.

Furthermore, being born out of wedlock opened the door to rejection. His mother hadn't yielded to an abortion—it "just wasn't the thing to do"—but neither she nor his teenage father really wanted a baby. He was an imposition on them both.

LEVEL THREE

Evan continued with his story:

My grandmother Edna had encouraged my mom to deliver me at home with a midwife. It was "the country thing to do" back then. But I was a breech birth, and problems required an emergency trip to the city hospital.

Dismantling Strongholds!

Identify → Repent, Renounce, Make Restitution → Bind Strongman → Spoil (Empty) His House → Evict Strongman → Glorify God!

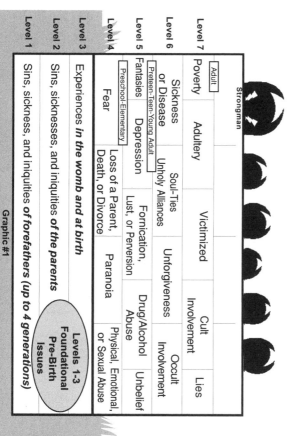

Strongman

Adult	Poverty	Adultery	Victimized	Cult Involvement	Lies
Preteen-Teen-Young Adult	Sickness or Disease	Unholy Alliances / Soul-Ties	Unforgiveness	Occult Involvement	
Preschool-Elementary	Fantasies / Depression	Fornication, Lust, or Perversion	Drug/Alcohol Abuse	Unbelief	
	Fear	Loss of a Parent, Death, or Divorce	Paranoia	Physical, Emotional, or Sexual Abuse	

Level 7
Level 6
Level 5
Level 4

Level 3 — Experiences *in the womb and at birth*

Level 2 — Sins, sicknesses, and iniquities *of the parents*

Level 1 — Sins, sickness, and iniquities *of forefathers (up to 4 generations)*

Levels 1-3 Foundational Pre-Birth Issues

Graphic #1
Chapter 8 - *Unravel the Strongman's Strength*
Copyright (c) 2006 Alice Smith

My mother always complained that she was so lonely during her pregnancy with me because Dad never saw her much, until my granddaddy insisted that they marry. So they married about two months before I was born.

Before Evan drew his first breath, he drew fear, isolation, trauma, and panic from his mother's womb.

LEVEL FOUR

The resentment between my parents must have been terrible. Even though I was too young to understand, I could sense something wasn't right between them.

When Evan was almost three, his daddy died in an automobile crash while drag-racing with friends. He had been restless and reckless, and although he hadn't wanted to be a father, he did try to accept Evan. But now he was gone.

And "gone" was the significant factor, for at three, Evan couldn't distinguish between his daddy's death and his daddy's rejection. His little mind simply registered, "Daddy didn't want me, so he left." Evan knew fear, abandonment, loneliness, and confusion. As *he* experienced it, this was the ultimate rejection.

Thereafter, Evan's aunt would keep him while his mother worked at the chicken processing plant. His mother, an uneducated teenager, had no idea how emotionally abusive her sister was to her son. Nor could she have known that her sister's husband physically abused Evan as well. And Evan? He would beg his mother not to take him there, but she didn't have a choice; he suffered in silence.

LEVEL FIVE

By the fifth and sixth grades, Evan was stealing alcohol from his grandfather, withdrawing from society, and escaping his pain through sexual fantasy. Grandmother Edna loved him most, and he knew it. But when she would tell him about the Lord's love and purpose for his life, he disconnected, even from her; the layers and layers of strongholds had formed a formidable wall. He simply couldn't believe that anyone, even God, truly loved him and wanted the best for him. His heart was filled with unbelief.

LEVEL SIX

Evan dropped out of high school at sixteen, disgusted with life, with people, and with himself. He was overcome with unforgiveness, suspicion, and bitterness. The pent-up rage inside was causing physical problems—headaches, dizziness, and a gnawing stomach were constant reminders of his troubled soul—but he ignored them.

Seeking to numb his anguish, Evan teamed up with guys actively involved in the occult. The supernatural fascinated him, and when he was told to drink blood to receive power, he was all for it. A strange sensation swept over him, causing Evan to believe he was finally in control.

Tragically, though, Evan's hopes for power were reversed, for demons soon controlled him. He was tormented by shadowy figures moving around his room at night. *What have I done?* he wondered.

His buddies offered assurance that their spiritual leader could heal the illnesses. But they were wrong. His pain was much more than skin deep. Evan left town to escape the nightmare of his occult involvement.

LEVEL SEVEN

Evan's misguided choices as a youth made him vulnerable to other cultic ideology. This time the deception revolved around a spiritual guru who was building an end-time commune with his followers' money. The pyramid scheme appeared harmless at first, and quick financial benefits convinced Evan he had made it in life. However, six months in, the government raided the property, shut down all accounts, and arrested the founder.

"My life has been wasted," Evan said regretfully. By the time he reached thirty he was facing financial ruin and had destroyed his first marriage through an affair with a colleague.

EVAN'S NEW LIFE

We were touched by Evan's life journey; at times it was hard for us not to cry. But then, like a flipped switch, his story changed. A broad grin broke across Evan's face as he said, "Finally, I found Christ." Though we often express it this way, the truth is, Christ wasn't lost! *Christ found Evan* on a Wednesday night service in a small Baptist church.

Earlier that evening, Evan had been sitting in his den, thinking about how lonely and empty he was. His heart ached with desperation. Then, in a flash, he remembered Grandmother Edna telling him about God's unconditional love. Needing answers, he immediately got up and went in search of a church.

Driving downtown, Evan spotted a church with cars parked around the building. He didn't hesitate to go inside, find a back-row seat, and begin listening to a young evangelist already into his sermon. Evan was mesmerized with his passion about the love of God. During the story of Jesus' sacrifice on the cross, Evan started to weep. When the preacher invited people to receive Christ, he dashed to be first at the front. That night he turned from his sin, repented for his rebellion against God, and asked Jesus Christ to be Lord of his life. He was born again! "I've never felt better in my life!" he gushed.

Evan had never known such love; just grief, fear, and rejection. Or such joy; just torment, lies, and confusion. Or such peace; just pain, sickness, and witchcraft. Now, at last, his sins were forgiven, and as far as he was concerned, he was in heaven—he couldn't imagine how it could get any better.

He was absolutely sure he'd spend eternity with God. And his nature— it was changing! Everyone seemed to see the difference, and many commented on it. He *was* different. Christ's life in him was evident in his attitudes, his desires, and his behavior.

"Why are you here to see us, Evan?" I asked. And he explained. Not long after receiving salvation, he sensed something was wrong: *something* lurked inside him, something that was especially angry about his decision for Christ. He said he was "coming unglued."

The more he sought God, the worse it got. The closer he'd get to God, the more turmoil he experienced. No matter what he did to compensate, his demons weren't about to give up easily. He needed help to gain freedom.

UNRAVELING AND DISMANTLING

STEP ONE: IDENTIFYING THE STRONGMEN

We prayed that God would give us revelation as to the source: "Heavenly Father, will you please reveal Evan's problem to all of us?" The insidious presence was a web of darkness that had tightly bound him with graveclothes of hopelessness. The strongholds had taken residence in his mind and body years before the Holy Spirit took up residence in his spirit. Now the war was on.

In our sessions with Evan, God spoke through His Word and through the revelatory gifts of the praying team members. (Revelatory gifts are prophecy, words of knowledge, discerning of spirits, etc., as put forward in 1 Corinthians 12. See also Acts 2:17–18; Romans 12:6; Hebrews 2:4.) Little by little, the Spirit disclosed the story you've just read.

With the Spirit's guidance and the aid of the "Apparent Demonic Groupings List," we were able to identify the three strongmen tormenting Evan's life. Then we reconstructed the process of how and where those spirits had entered. The Lord showed us the "pillar events" (entry points) the enemy had used to gain toeholds that had become footholds that eventually grew into strongholds.

STEP TWO: REPENTANCE

Next we guided Evan to pray in repentance, one issue at a time. This step was not just to acknowledge that he had committed sin (which was a foregone conclusion), and it wasn't only to ask for God's forgiveness, since God had forgiven him the moment he had trusted Christ as Savior. This was more about *agreeing with God about what God had done*. It was about *thanking the Lord for His forgiveness and cleansing*, therefore leveling the playing field against evil spirits who desperately wanted to keep their stronghold intact.

Then Evan repented for the sins of his parents and forefathers (see Nehemiah 1:6–7; Psalm 106:6–8; Jeremiah 14:20). Not that he was actually personally guilty of their sins, but he was representative of them. Mending the cracks in the past's foundations, he effectively apologized for what his predecessors had done to offend the Lord and separate themselves from Him. When he released himself of their judgment against him, he instantly sensed relief.

STEP THREE: RENUNCIATION

After repenting, Evan acknowledged the areas in which he'd cooperated with darkness, and he renounced any involvement he'd had with the enemy. We ended with homework for Evan to do before our next session.

He was to make three lists: a list of positions he held (son, employee, brother, friend, etc.), a list of the sins God would bring to his remembrance, and a list recording everything he owned. Then, from the lists, he was to read aloud each item and surrender it—position, sin, or possession—to the Lord. He was to close with a total surrender of everything he is and has to the Lord Jesus Christ. (Remember: Deliverance can involve truth encounters *and* power encounters; the demonic grip can continue to loosen through both as we peel off the dark layers of the past.)

STEP FOUR: RESTITUTION AND RECONCILIATION

By the next meeting Evan had turned his attention to those he'd cheated and/or to whom he'd lied. I instructed him to make phone calls, to return stolen property, and to make arrangements to pay back anyone he'd disadvantaged. He agreed; we would meet again after he obeyed all the Lord had shown him to do. As we spent time encouraging him with biblical promises and speaking life into his future, several team members shared prophetic words, a source of great joy for him.

STEP FIVE: BINDING THE STRONGMAN

A week later, when we reconvened and continued, we sought the Lord for specific guidance: "Father, put your finger on what you want us to deal with." Evan's eyes flickered, and his body shook violently; all the while his teeth chattered as if he were chilled to the bone. (By the way, the devil is crafty but never original. Through many years of helping people in deliverance I've noticed the enemy using the same patterns and methods over and over.)

"I bind every strongman right now. Starting with fear. Spirit of fear, I know who you are. God has given you into my hands. I bind you now and command you powerless." (Keep your eyes open. You can't discern what's happening with your eyes closed.)

"Spirit of heaviness and spirit of witchcraft, I bind you by the ambassadorial authority given me by Christ Jesus" (see Matthew 10:1; Mark 6:7; Luke 10:19). "Devils, you are uncovered, and your stronghold will be vacated."

STEP SIX: EMPTYING THE STRONGMAN'S HOUSE

Once we'd bound the strongman, we carefully and methodically "emptied his house" or, as Jesus said, "spoil[ed] his goods." I addressed the lesser spirits that supported and served the strongman. Evan jerked onto the floor, screaming, "No, no, no!" I ordered the defeated demons to "shut up and come out of him."

MATTERS TO KEEP IN MIND

As you are beginning to cast out the demons, you might want to read the list in the first appendix, considering the spirits under each strongman category. Pause if a demon apparently is hesitating to leave; then, firmly rebuke it again. Continue down the list. You might say, "The strongman can't help you, demons. He's bound and helpless. You will obey me, so get out. I'm now cleaning the house of fear."

Now move to the next strongman: "Spirit of heaviness, you are bound. Everything in the stronghold of heaviness is leaving." (Wait for assurance from the Lord—not relying on the presence of manifestations—to know that breakthrough is occurring.) "Witchcraft, your house is falling, so leave."

Continue in this manner to pursue deliverance. Remember that there can be another set of three strongmen (and their networks) attached to a person. This is dependent on the level of sin he or she was involved in.

- Don't be intimidated or threatened by demons. Never speak aloud that you don't know what to do. Devils will take advantage of your inexperience if you confess your weakness.
- Don't listen to them; they are liars.
- Command them to shut up, obey you, and then get out and never return.
- Sometimes it's necessary to get the person involved by having him rise

up and command the spirits to loose him, by repeating aloud the rebuke you are saying.

- No one, including me, can tell you how many devils you will have to cast out of a person.
- Always, always depend solely on the Holy Spirit for revelation.
- Never slap, humiliate, punch, or embarrass the one you are helping. If he is confused with the process, stop and explain you aren't angry with him but with the demons that have tormented him.
- Be flexible. Even the most skilled ministers have difficult deliverances at times.

STEP SEVEN: EVICTING THE STRONGMAN

Again, after the house is empty of lesser demons, *then* we cast out the strongman. "Witchcraft, now we command you to leave Evan's life, in the name of Jesus."

Without much struggle, and with a whimper, the spirit of witchcraft left. The demonic spirits that strengthened witchcraft were gone and without their help, the strongman couldn't stand. As a mental picture, it was as though witchcraft had been standing atop a demonic pyramid; when his props were knocked out from beneath him, he had nothing on which to stand. Witchcraft was almost glad to depart from Evan!

When the strongholds had been emptied, and when the bosses of each stronghold of the house had been kicked out, it was over. Our team knew it, and Evan knew it. Peace flooded his countenance.

At this point, we asked the Lord to minister strength to Evan and to close all doors in his life where the enemy had taken advantage. We prayed for his inner man (his spirit) to be strong and surrendered to hear and obey the Lord. We asked the Lord to increase Evan's desire to learn the Word and to walk in purity and holiness. We prayed a hedge of protection over his relationships, his possessions, and his home.

Evan committed to remain in a Bible-believing church, to tithe, to pray, and to walk in accountability with godly people. It was awesome to see the glorious freedom he received. And all for the right purpose: the glory of God!

CHAPTER 9

Clean but Empty!

My first encounter with demons was hair-raising*! In 1970, few people worked in the area of deliverance, and, coming from an evangelical background, neither Eddie nor I had any experience with the demonic. We'd been taught since childhood that biblical references to demons were merely first-century expressions for mental illness.*

We were at a revival meeting in central Texas when our eyes of understanding were opened. God truly visited this church and city, and within a few days genuine revival had come. In the midnight hours, people came spontaneously to the church and wept until morning. Lives were dramatically converted during those days of wondrous visitation. When the Lord began to deal with sin in our hearts, the darkness in us couldn't stay hidden.

Looking back on it now, I can't help but be amazed at how naïve I was about spiritual darkness. One woman, a key leader in this large metropolitan church, stood out to me because she told us she knew fourteen of the twenty-seven New Testament books from memory. Right away when I met Jane, she began to quote Scripture. I was impressed, and I instantly admired her.

However, after one service, when several of us were talking, Jane seemed to completely change personalities. Then she crudely announced that she had to leave to "go home to feed 'Dumb-Dumb'" (meaning her husband). At first I thought she was joking—but she was serious! An eerie fire in her eyes sent cold chills up my spine. I knew I wasn't experienced in the things of God, but discernment, I had—and I knew this wasn't right.

After another service we were asked to join the evangelist and the pastor to pray for Jane. (I don't recall the events or circumstances that led to her ending up in the pastor's office.) Words can't fully describe what I saw and experienced the three weeks we ministered to her, mostly after morning or evening services. This much I can say: I've never seen a person so demonized, before or since.

During an opening prayer Jane began to growl like a dog. When the minister challenged the demons in her, she leapt forward, lunging from a sitting position about fifteen feet away. Whoa! Humans don't do this on their own, and immediately I realized there was something supernaturally unnatural at hand.

I sat to Jane's left, nervously trying not to act worried. (This was all so new to me; I honestly was scared to death.) When she growled like a lion, from deep within her belly, I almost lost it! Then, without warning, the demonized woman flung her left hand outward, hitting my leg. Before you could count to three, I was out of my chair, running down the stairs toward the altar. Fast on my heels was a pastor friend from Louisiana, at least as freaked out as I was. My upbringing hadn't prepared me to see this, and my emotions had gotten the best of me.

Day after day the battle raged. Evil spirits were fighting to stay, and the pastor was commanding them to leave. In those weeks we saw many demonic manifestations. Nonetheless, the entire team learned the most important dimension of delivering captives: *Jane had never been born again.* For several weeks we fought and fought and fought, until one day the evangelist stopped the ministry and asked Jane about her salvation experience.

She described it as having heard a strange voice in her left ear saying, "Let me be your lord!" She never questioned the voice—she assumed it was God, and she embraced it. After she submitted, everything in her life changed for the worse. She would erupt in rage without reason or warning. She had dark thoughts about death and blood.

The evangelist and the pastor explained to her how the Holy Spirit convicts of sin. It was clear that the Lord was already working in her heart. Right away she began to cry. Her repentance of sin and renunciation of the demonic were so precious. Once Jane surrendered her heart to Christ, deliverance became much easier.

This brings me to my main point: I never minister deliverance to one who is lost unless the person is willing to receive Christ. You may want freedom for your friend, your spouse, your child, but unless and until they want freedom for themselves, you may actually be doing them a disservice. Again, Jesus gives us this warning:

> When the unclean spirit is gone out of a man, he walketh through dry places, seeking rest, and findeth none. Then he saith, I will return into my house from whence I came out; and when he is come, he findeth it empty, swept, and garnished.
>
> Then goeth he, and taketh with himself seven other spirits more wicked than himself, and they enter in and dwell there: and the last state of that man is worse than the first. Even so shall it be also unto this wicked generation. (Matthew 12:43–45)

Note that the demons say, "I will return into my house." A house is a place of comfort and familiarity. Ridding a person of demons is only half the job. Seeing that one filled with the Spirit of Christ is the other half. Without this, he or she will be *clean, but empty*.

When the person *is* born again, maintaining his or her freedom is crucial. Paul told Timothy, "Hold fast the pattern of sound words which you have heard from me, in faith and love which are in Christ Jesus. That good thing which was committed to you, keep by the Holy Spirit who dwells in us" (2 Timothy 1:13–14 NKJV). Let's look at a strategy to maintain your victory. When you minister to others, teach them these guidelines as well.

GUIDELINES FOR MAINTENANCE

(1) DESIRE FREEDOM

To maintain your deliverance, ask the Lord to create an inner longing and a state of mind that will keep you focused on Him. No one can force you to do the right things or to keep you craving freedom. Spend dedicated time with the Lord in prayer and in Bible study. Invest in relationships with godly people who will provide a mutual support system of positive reinforcement.

Choose to walk in freedom. Don't assume that old habits of bondage will fall away on their own, by default. Charles Swindoll once wrote,

> *A war [the American Civil War] had been fought—the bloodiest in our history. A president had been assassinated. An amendment to the Constitution had been signed into law. Once-enslaved men, women, and children were now legally emancipated. Yet amazingly, many continued living in fear and squalor as though it had never happened. In a context of hard-earned freedom, slaves chose to remain as slaves.*[1]

Once free of the demonic, don't continue to live as though you're still enslaved.

If you find yourself fighting through a familiar weakness, this doesn't necessarily mean bondage has returned. Don't let a "struggle" turn to despair or acceptance of this issue. Stay on the offensive; in prayer get God's perspective about your struggle, submit this to Christ, and regain your peace.

(2) STAY DETERMINED

A desire for freedom, alone, isn't enough: you must be determined not to lose what you've found. Paul exhorts Timothy to *hold fast* the Scriptures, to the substance of unfailing truth in them. It is not enough to assent to the sound words—we must also love them. The Christian faith is a trust committed to us; it is of unspeakable value in itself, and it will be of indescribable advantage to us. The Word is committed to us to be preserved, pure and entire, yet we must not think to keep it by our own strength but by the power of the Holy Spirit dwelling in us; it will not be gained by those who trust in their own heart and lean on their own understanding.

(3) AVOID CARELESSNESS

Once you've experienced freedom, the devil will return to test you, attempting to try to take back the ground he's lost. Satan is a sore and sorry loser, so be prepared to be challenged. Carelessness with where you go, what you do, and whom you're with can reopen doors you've asked God to shut on your behalf. I'm not trying to scare you, but when it comes to freedom or bondage, why be thoughtless about your freedom? Be determined to run from anything or anyone that leads you astray. The stronghold that's been in you is a weakness you may deal with to some degree until memories of the old life subside and new memories are recorded.

I remember Eddie leading a Christian man through deliverance from alcohol (spirit of bondage). This man had experienced radical change within a short period of time, and he was riding high on the strength that he felt. During one of their counseling sessions, he bragged to Eddie about keeping alcohol in a drawer at his office to remind him he didn't need it any longer. Eddie warned him that his actions were careless, nothing more than a potential open door for the stronghold once more to take advantage of him at a time of weakness.

This man was sure his "self-challenge" was both harmless and helpful, and he tried to convince Eddie of it. A few months later he suffered the painful loss of a parent, and, in his weakness, he drank the liquor he'd kept within his reach. Fortunately he didn't remain there—he quickly repented of his sin and didn't touch alcohol again.

Remember, a stronghold is something we are familiar with, and it feels more normal and safe to allow it access than to pursue and maintain faith and freedom. So beware.

(4) STAY IN THE WORD OF GOD

"Your word is a lamp to my feet and a light to my path" (Psalm 119:105). There's a reason the Word is grafted into us when we receive it. If you are hiding the Word in your heart, it will be much less likely that you will fall into sin or succumb to the strongholds of the past.

Consider reading aloud the "Sweet P's" of the Twenty-third psalm to yourself for a season of time.

- *Possession:* The Lord is my Shepherd.
- *Provision:* I shall not want.

- *Position:* You make me to lie down.
- *Progress:* You lead me.
- *Personal:* You restore my soul.
- *Purpose:* For your name's sake.
- *Peace:* I will fear no evil.
- *Protection:* You are with me.
- *Pilgrimage:* Your rod and staff, they comfort me.
- *Participation:* You prepare a table before me.
- *Preparation:* You anoint my head with oil.
- *Plenty:* My cup runs over.
- *Preservation:* Surely goodness and mercy shall follow me all the days of my life.
- *Place:* And I will dwell in the house of the Lord forever.[2]

(5) MAINTAIN HEALTHY SELF-TALK

Stay spiritually healthy by speaking to yourself with psalms and hymns and spiritual songs (see Ephesians 5:19). Praise is an outward expression of an inward attitude. Declare aloud the great things the Lord is doing for you. Let other healthy people speak goodness and encouragement into your life. Remind yourself that you aren't the person you once were, and celebrate your liberty with elaborate praise to God.

Psychologists tell us that the average person speaks forty to fifty thousand things to her/himself daily, 70 percent or more of which are negative. *However, the most exceptional professional athletes are said to reduce their self-talk to twenty thousand or fewer statements, and less than 50 percent are negative.*[3]

As Christians we are seasonal. For example, in the "spring" of our walk with God, when the flowers are budding and we see the sun shining brightly, we know and feel that life is good. Later we might go through the "autumn," when God is convicting us of sin, issues are coming to the surface, and the Lord is sloughing off the junk in our life. This is part of God's way to develop purity in us.

We especially need to know that this doesn't mean we've become entangled again with strongholds. Rather than assuming that struggle means you're failing, affirm it as an invitation to heal and grow. Being conformed into Christ's likeness means we *will* have areas of ongoing progress until we're completely like Him. Until then, there will always be opportunities for growth.

(6) REMAIN TEACHABLE

Teachable people allow others to speak truth into their lives. This attitude allows our narrow way of looking at things to be broadened by revelation. I heard an old preacher say from the pulpit, "This is the worst time in the history of the Christian church for a person to be a know-it-all." He's right. The moment we close the door to learning, we're in jeopardy of being legalistic, self-righteous, and self-focused. This is nothing more than pride, which always goes before destruction (Proverbs 16:18). It's critical that we have an attitude of always learning, always being open to correction, always being willing to seek God, that we may be fruitful stewards of what He's given us. We are to be "rooted and built up in him, and established in the faith, as [we] have been taught, abounding therein with thanksgiving" (Colossians 2:7).

(7) BE FILLED WITH THE HOLY SPIRIT

When we're filled with the Spirit, we can't be filled with ourselves. The truth is, whatever is inside will come out! To be filled with the Spirit, we must be emptied of self.

If I showed you a lemon and asked, "What's in this lemon?" you'd answer, "Lemon juice." Not necessarily. What if I had replaced the lemon juice with sugar water? Whatever *is* inside will come out when we're peeled or squeezed!

Repent of sin. Surrender to the lordship of Jesus Christ. Ask the Holy Spirit to come and baptize you in the fire of God's holiness and fill you with himself.

A devout woman was asked how she knew the Spirit's voice. She answered, "How do you know your husband's step and your child's cry from the step and cry of others? I can't tell you how I know the voice of the Spirit, but it's as real to me as the voice of any other person I know." If we are "filled with the Spirit," "live in the Spirit," and "walk in the Spirit," we will be familiar with the Spirit. (See Ephesians 5:18; Galatians 5:16, 25.) Abiding in Christ, we can know spiritual intimacy with Him as real as that of our dearest loved one.

Clean but empty? No! We can be clean and filled with God.

APPARENT DEMONIC GROUPINGS LIST

ALTAR MINISTRY RESOURCE DEMONIC GROUPINGS

DEAF AND DUMB SPIRIT

Accidents

Blindness—Matt. 12:22

Burning accidents—Mark 9:22

Crying, uncontrolled**—Matt.
15:23; Mark 9:26

Confusion—James 3:16

Convulsions

Deafness—Ps. 38:13–14

Death—Prov. 6:16–19

Destruction—Lev. 26:21–22

Drowning accidents—Mark 9:22

Dumbness (in the Greek,
"insanity")—Mark 9:25

Ear infection, chronic—Mark
9:25–26

Emotionless

Epilepsy—Matt. 17:15–18

Eye diseases—Lev. 26:16

Fear of:
Fire—Isa. 4:4
Water

Foaming at mouth—Luke 9:39;
Mark 9:18–20

Gnashing of teeth—Mark 9:18

Infections (chronic)

Insanity

Lethargy

Lunatic behavior—Mark 9:20

Madness—Deut. 28:34; John 10:20

Motionless stupor

Pining away—Isa. 38:12; Mark
9:18

Poverty—Prov. 6:9–11

Schizophrenia

Seizures—Mark 9:18, 20, 26

Self-pity

Sensing the "approach of death"

Sleepiness—Prov. 20:13; Matt. 25:5

Stuttering

Stupors

Suicide—Mark 9:22

Tearing—Mark 9:18, 26, 29

Turrets—Job 16:9; Mark 9:18

Unbelief—Heb. 3:12

Unforgiveness—Luke 6:37

Wallowing—2 Peter 2:22

Note:

** For uncontrolled crying, also see Spirit of Heaviness

BIND	LOOSE
▸ Deaf and Dumb Spirit—Mark 9:25; Matt. 17:15	▸ Healing—Mal. 4:2; Acts 10:38 ▸ Hearing—Rom. 10:17 ▸ Boldness—Eph. 3:12

FAMILIAR SPIRIT
Witchcraft; Spirit of Divination

Astrology—Isa. 47:13
Automatic handwriting
Channeling
Charmer—Deut. 18:11
Charms (good luck)
Clairvoyance—1 Sam. 28:7–8
Conjuring (summoning demons to appear)—Isa. 44:25
Consulter of dead—Deut. 18:11; 1 Chron. 10:13

Cults (False Religions and Belief Systems):
  Belial
  Black Panthers
  Buddhism
  Catholicism (anything unbiblical therein)
  Christian Science
  Confucianism
  Freemasonry
  Hinduism
  Islam
  Jehovah's Witnesses (Watchtower)
  KKK
  Mind Control
  Mormonism
  Rosicrucianism
  Satanism
  Scientology
  Shintoism
  Taoism
  Theosophy
  Unitarianism
  Unity
  Universalism
  Witchcraft

Disobedience—Rom. 1:30; Heb. 4:6
Divination—Jer. 29:8; Hosea 4:12
Doctrinal error—Lev. 19:31
Doctrinal obsession—1 Tim. 1:3–7
Dreamer (False Dreams)**—Jer. 23:32; 27:9–10
Drugs—Rev. 21:8; 22:15; Gal. 5:20
Easily persuaded—Prov. 2:12–13
Enchanter—Deut. 18:12; Isa. 19:3
False prophecies***—Isa. 8:19; 29:4; Deut. 13:1–3
Family curses—Gen. 4:11; Isa. 14:21; Jer. 32:18
Fantasy

Fear of:
  God (unhealthy)
  Hell
  Losing salvation

Fetishes (good-luck pieces)
Formalism
Fortune-telling—Micah 5:12; Isa. 2:6; Lev. 20:6
Generational iniquity—Isa. 1:4; Matt. 27:25; John 9:1–3
Hallucinations—Rev. 21:8; 22:15
Handwriting analysis
Harlotry—Lev. 20:6
Horoscope—Matt. 16:2–4; Isa. 47:13; Lev. 19:26; Jer. 10:2
Hypnosis

Idolatry—Hosea 4:12

Incantation

Incest—2 Sam. 13:14

Incubus or Succubus (unseen demon spirits)—Gen. 6:2–4

Lawlessness—1 John 3:4; 2 Thess. 1:7–8

Legalism—Gal. 1:1–7; 1 Tim. 4:1–3

Lethargy—Prov.20:4

Levitation

Liar—1 Tim. 1:10

Magic, black/white—Ex. 7:11, 22; 8:7; Lev. 19:26

Manipulation—Titus 1:9–10

Medium—1 Sam. 28:7

Mind control—Jer. 23:16, 25, 32

Mind reading

Music that defies, mocks, or rejects God

Muttering

Necromancy (consulting the dead)—Deut. 18:11

New Age philosophies and involvement

Obsessions

Occultism—2 Chron. 33:6

Ouija board

Palmistry

Passive mind

Pendulum divination

Poverty—Prov. 6:6–11

Rebellion—1 Sam. 15:22

Religiosity—Job 15:4–6

Ritualism

Satanism

Séance

Seduction—Prov. 9:13–18

Self-will—Prov. 1:25–30

Soothsayer—Micah 5:12; Isa. 2:6; Jer. 27:9–10

Sorcery—Mic. 5:12–15

Spirit guide(s)

Spiritism—1 Sam. 28; Lev. 20:6

Stubbornness—Lev. 26:15

Superficial spirituality—2 Tim. 2:17–18

Suspicion

Tarot cards

Trance

Witch, witchcraft—Lev. 19:26; 20:6; Deut. 18:10

Consider Also:

Conjuring

I Ching

Hiphop music

Jewelry, occult

Martial Arts

Mental telepathy

Movies, horror

Past-life readings

Pokémon

Psychic healing

Reike

Rock music

Spiritual adultery (spiritual unfaithfulness)

Superstition

Tea leaves

Transcendental Meditation

Victim

Voodoo

Yoga

Notes:

**For Dreamer, also see Lying Spirit and Spirit of Heaviness

***For False Prophecies, also see Lying Spirit

BIND	LOOSE
▸ Familiar Spirit, Spirit of Divination—Acts 16:16–18; Deut. 18:11; Lev. 20:6, 27; 1 Chron. 10:13	▸ Truth—Ps. 15:1–2; Prov. 3:3; John 8:32; 2 Cor. 13:8 ▸ Revelation—Gal. 1:12; Eph. 1:17

HAUGHTY SPIRIT (PRIDEFUL SPIRIT)

Agitated—Titus 3:3

Angry—Prov. 29:22

Argumentative

Arrogant—Jer. 48:29; Isa. 2:11, 17; 5:15; 2 Sam. 22:28

Boastful—Eph. 2:8–9; 2 Tim. 3:2

Bitter—James 3:14

Bragging—2 Peter 2:18

Competitive, excessively

Condescending

Contentious—Prov. 13:10

Controlling

Covetous—2 Peter 2:18

Critical—Matt. 7:1

Deception—Heb. 3:12–13

Dictatorial

Domineering

Education, pride of or preoccupation with—Titus 3:9–11

Egocentric—Job 41:34

Egotistical

Elitist

Entitlement

False humility

Frustration

Gossip—2 Cor. 12:20

Greed—Rom. 1:29–30; 1 Tim. 6:10

Hatred—Prov. 26:26

Haughtiness—2 Peter 2:10

Holier-than-thou attitude

Idleness—Ezra 16:49–50

Impatience

Importance

Insolence—2 Tim. 3:3

Intellectualism—1 Tim. 1:4, 6–7

Intolerance

Irritability—Phil. 2:14

Judgmentalism—Matt. 7:1

Liar—Prov. 19:22; 1 Tim. 1:9–10

Lofty looks

Mocker—Ps. 35:16

Obstinacy—Prov. 29:1; Dan. 5:20

Overbearing

Perfectionist

Playacting

Pretension

Pride—Prov. 6:16–17; 16:18; Isa. 28:1

Rage—Prov. 6:34; Gal. 5:19

Rationalism

Rebellion—1 Sam. 15:23; Prov. 29:1

Rejection of God (atheism)— 1 John 2:22

Religious spirit

Resentment—Ex. 8:15

Scornful—Prov. 1:22; 3:34; 21:24; 29:8

Self-centeredness—James 3:14

Self-deception—Jer. 49:16; Obad. 1:3

Self-delusion—Rev. 3:17

Self-importance

Self-pity

Self-righteousness—Isa. 64:6; Luke 18:11–12

Selfish—Gal. 5:19

Smug—2 Sam. 22:28; Jer. 48:29

Stiff-necked—Ex. 32:9; Acts 7:51

Stubborn—Ps. 81:11

Superiority

Theatrics

Uncompassionate

Unforgiveness—Matt. 18:35

Unkind

Vanity—Ps. 119:113; 2 Peter 2:18

Violent—Ps. 7:16

Wrath**

Note:
**For Wrath, see Jealousy

BIND	LOOSE
▸ Haughty/Prideful Spirit—Prov. 6:16–18; 16:18; 21:24; Isa. 16:6; Eccl. 7:8	▸ Humility—1 Peter 5:5; Ps. 10:17; Prov. 22:4; 29:23 ▸ Mercy—James 2:13; 1 Peter 2:10, Jude 1:2

LYING SPIRIT

Accusations—Rev. 12:10; Ps. 31:18

Adultery—2 Peter 2:14; Prov. 6:32

Apostasy—2 Peter 2:1–3

Arguments—2 Tim. 2:23–24

Arrogance—Isa. 2:11

Cheating

Crying—Matt. 15:23

Curses—Num. 5:24

Deceit—Ps. 101:7; 2 Thess. 2:9–13
Delusions, strong—Isa. 66:4
Depraved desires
Divination—Jer. 29:8
Doctrines, false—1 Tim. 4:1; Heb.
13:9
Dreamer
Drivenness, excessive
Drugs
Emotionalism
Exaggeration
False:
 Burdens
 Compassion
 Doctrines
 Oaths—Ps. 144:8; Ezek. 21:23
 Prophets—Isa. 9:15
 Prophecy**—Jer. 23:16–17;
 27:9–10
 Responsibility
 Spirituality
 Teaching
 Witness—Prov. 19:5; Matt.
 15:19; Mark 10:19
Fear of authority
Financial problems (especially with
 tithing)
Flattery—Prov. 26:28; 29:5
Gossip—2 Tim. 2:16; Prov. 20:19
Heresy—1 Cor. 11:19; Gal. 5:20
Homosexuality***—Rom. 1:26
Hypocrisy—Isa. 32:6; 1 Tim. 4:2
Insinuations
Jezebel Spirit—Rev. 2:20; 1 Kings
 18:4–13; 19:1–2
Lies—2 Chron. 18:22; Prov. 6:16–
 19
Lust—Ps. 81:12; Rom. 1:27

Mental bondage—Rom. 8:15; Heb.
2:15
Mind control
Passion, inordinate—Deut. 32:5
Perfectionist
Performance
Poverty—Mal. 3:8–12; Ps. 34:9–10
Pride—Prov. 16:18; Isa. 28:3
Profanity
Rationalization
Religious spirit—Job 8:3–7
Robbery—Ex. 20:15; Prov. 1:10–14
Seeking of approval (insecurity)
Self-image (feel worthless, ugly,
 hopeless)
Self-inflicted curses—Deut. 28:15;
 1 Kings 18:28
Sexual:
 Adultery—1 Cor. 6:9–11
 Fantasies—Prov. 23:26–28
 Fornication
 Homosexual behavior—Rom.
 1:26–27
 Lesbianism—Rom. 1:26–27
 Masturbation—Gen 38:9
 Pornography
 Sodomy****
 Transsexual behavior—
 1 Cor. 6:9
 Transvestite—Rom. 1:26–27
Slander—Prov. 10:18; Rom. 12:17
Superstitions—Acts 17:22
Talking, excessive—1 Tim. 6:20
Uncleanness—Eph. 5:3–4
Vain imaginations—Deut. 29:19;
 Rom. 1:21; 2 Cor. 10:5
Vanity—Job 15:3 1

Vengeance—Rom. 12:19   Wickedness—Rom. 1:29
Victim

Notes:
** For False Prophecy, also see Familiar Spirit
*** For Homosexuality, also see Whoredom and Perversion
**** For Sodomy, also see Whoredom and Perversion

BIND	LOOSE
▸ Lying Spirit—2 Chron. 18:22; 1 Kings 22:22–23; 2 Thess. 2:7–12	▸ Honesty—1 Tim. 2:2; Prov. 16:11; Phil. 4:8 ▸ Goodness—Ps. 23:6; 2 Thess. 1:11; Eph. 5:9

SEDUCING SPIRIT

Attracted to false prophets, signs and wonders—Jer. 14:14; Matt. 24:24
Deceived—Prov. 24:28
Easily swayed—2 Tim. 3:6
Emulation—Gal. 5:19–21
Exploitation—Prov. 9:13–18
Fascination with evil ways, evil objects, and evil persons
Fear of man
Greedy—Prov. 1:19
Gullibility

Hypocritical lies—Matt. 6:2; 1 Peter 2:1
Music that defies, mocks, or rejects God
Seared conscience—1 Tim. 4:2
Seduced, enticed—2 Tim. 3:6; Eph. 4:14–16
Seeks attention
Sensual in dress, actions—Prov. 9:3–5
Trance
Wanders from the truth of God—2 Tim. 4:3–4

BIND	LOOSE
▸ Seducing Spirit—1 Tim. 4:1; Mark 13:22; 2 Tim. 3:13;	▸ Spirit of Truth—John 14:17; 15:26; 1 John 4:6 ▸ Spirit of Holiness—Rom 1:4; Eph. 4:24; 1 Peter 1:16

SHADOW OF DEATH

Abandons friends or family—
1 Sam. 12:22
Aching heart
Blinded heart and mind—Acts
28:27
Deception—Isa. 8:19
Depression—Isa. 61:3
Despair—Isa. 61:1
Discouragement
Dreams of being attacked by:
Animals
Demons
Grim Reaper
Dreams of:
Being chased by dead people
Being flogged
Being hit by a vehicle
Being married to dead people
Being shot
Falling into a pit and being
unable to get out
Walking in a graveyard
Excessive mourning or grief—Isa.
61:3
Fear—2 Tim. 1:7

Hopelessness
Isolation
Lethargy
Mental torment
Murder—1 Tim. 1:9
Obsession with:
Blood
Death—Prov. 2:17–18
Violence
Oppression—Job 35:9; Prov. 3:31
Seduction—Prov. 2:16–18
Seeing shadowy, dark figure
Self-affliction—1 Kings 18:28
Sharp pains in the body—Prov.
14:30
Something keeps whispering that
he or she is going to die
Sickness or disease that doesn't
respond to prayers or medical
treatment—Prov. 14:30
Sorrow—Isa. 35:10
Sudden loss of appetite
Suicide
Thoughts of suicide—Ps. 103:4

BIND	LOOSE
▸ Shadow of Death—Isa. 28:15; Ps. 23:4; 44:19, 107:10–14	▸ Life—Rom. 8:2, 11; John 10:9–10 ▸ Light—Dan. 5:14; Ps. 112:4; 1 John 2:8; 1 Peter 2:9; Eph. 1:18

SPIRIT OF ANTICHRIST

Acts against the miracles of God

Acts against the Word of God—
Titus 2:5

Against Christ and His teachings—
2 Thess. 2:4; 1 John 4:3

Against Christians—Acts 17:13

Against God—Isa. 52:5

Attacks the saints—Acts 9:1

Attacks the testimony of Christ

Attempts to rationalize Christ

Attempts to take Christ's place

Blasphemes Holy Spirit—Mark
3:29; Luke 12:10; 1 Tim. 1:20

Closed-mindedness

Confusion—James 3:16; 1 Cor.
14:33

Critical—Prov. 16:28

Cults**

Deceiver—1 John 2:18–26; Rom.
7:11; 2 Thess. 2:4, 10; 2 John 7

Defensiveness

Denies the atonement—1 John 4:3;
2 John 7–8

Denies the blood of Christ

Denies the deity of Christ—Matt.
26:63–64

Denies the work of the Holy Spirit

Displays open unbelief

Disturbs fellowship and gathering
of the saints

Doctrinal error/twisting of doctrine—Isa. 19:14; Rom. 1:22–23;
2 Tim. 3:7–8; Acts 13:10;
2 Peter 2:14

Explains away the miracles of God

Harasses/persecutes the saints

Humanism

Ignores and opposes Christ's blood

Judgmentalism

Lawlessness—2 Thess. 2:7

Legalism—1 Tim. 4:3

Mean-spirited—Prov. 1:19

Mocking attitude

Occult—Acts 16:16–21

Opposes

Bible

Blood of Christ

Deity of Christ—1 John 4:3

Doctrine of Christ—2 Tim. 3:8
Fellowship of Christ
Humanity of Christ
Miracles
Men of God—Rev. 13:7; Dan.
   7:21
The Ministry
Victory of Christ
Persecutes the saints

Rationalizes the Word—Prov. 3:7–8
Self-exalting—2 Cor. 10:12–13;
   1 Tim. 3:6
Stirs up strife between believers—
   1 Cor. 3:3
Suppresses ministry—Matt. 23:13
Violent—Prov. 16:29
Worldliness—1 John 4:5

Note
**For Cults, also see Familiar Spirit

BIND	LOOSE
▶ Spirit of Antichrist—1 John 4:3; 2 Thess. 2:4	▶ Christ—Acts 15:11, 16:31; 1 Peter 4:16; Rom. 1:16 ▶ Grace—Rom. 1:5; 6:14; Gal. 6:18; Eph. 4:7

SPIRIT OF BONDAGE

Accusation—Rev. 12:10; Col. 3:5
Addictions:
   Alcohol
   Caffeine
   Cigarettes/Nicotine
   Drugs (legal or illegal)
   Food
   Medications (above and beyond
      prescribed use)
   Sex—Ezek. 16:28–29
Anguish of spirit—Rom. 2:9
Anorexia
Anxiety—Phil. 4:6–7

Bitterness—Eph. 4:31
Bound
Bulimia
Broken-hearted—Ps. 51:17
Bruised spirit—Ezek. 23:3
Compulsive behavior—Prov. 5:22;
   John 8:34
Compulsory subjection and control
Condemnation—2 Cor. 3:9
Coveting wealth in order to hoard
   it—Luke 12:16–21
Critical spirit—1 Peter 2:1
Death wish—Isa. 8:19

Dominance
Doubting salvation—2 Cor. 13:5
Drivenness, excessive
Embarrassment
False burden
False compassion
False guilt
False humility—Gal. 6:3
False responsibility
Fault-finding
Fear of death—Heb. 2:14–15
Fears—Rom. 8:15
Feeling "lost"
Frustration
Helplessness
Hopelessness—Prov. 13:12
Hyperactivity
Inability to break free—Isa. 58:6
Idleness—Prov. 19:15
Gluttony—1 Cor. 6:12–13; 2 Tim. 3:3–4; Phil. 3:19
Judgmentalism—Isa. 28:6; Rom. 14:13
Lostness—Heb. 2:3

Maladies and forms of sickness:
ADD/ADHD
Chronic Fatigue Syndrome
MPD
Paranoia
Phantom pain (not due to loss of a limb)

Schizophrenia
Turret's Syndrome
Medications, hooked on
Mind control
Nervousness
No assurance of salvation
Oppression—Acts 10:32
Perfectionism
Possessiveness
Poverty—Ps. 34:9–10
Rejection—Judges 11:2–3
Resentment**
Restlessness—Isa. 28:12
Satanism—Acts 26:18
Self-condemnation—Job 9:20–21
Self-deception—Gal. 6:3
Self-pity
Self-reward (overeating, etc.)
Shame—Rev. 3:18
Slavery—Rom. 6:15–16
Spiritual blindness—2 Cor. 4:3–4
Stiffness—Acts 7:51
Strife—Gal. 5:19–20
Suicide—Matt. 27:5
Superiority
Uncontrolled spending
Unholy soul-ties—Matt. 5:27–28; Acts 5:1–4
Unrighteousness—1 Peter 2:12
Vagabond spirit—Ps. 109:10; Acts 19:13; 1 Tim. 5:13
Witchcraft—Nah. 3:4; Gal. 5:20
Worthlessness—Ps. 4:2

Note:
**For Resentment, also see Spirit of Jealousy

BIND	LOOSE
▸ Spirit of Bondage—Rom. 8:15; Gal. 4:3, 5:1	▸ Liberty—Rom. 8:21; Gal. 5:13 ▸ Spirit of Adoption—Rom. 8:15, 28

SPIRIT OF ERROR

Always right—Ps. 36:1
Angry—Prov. 29:22
Argumentative—1 Tim. 1:10
Competitive, excessively
Contentious—1 Tim. 5:13
Cults/Occult—Acts 16
Defensiveness
Doctrines of devils—1 Tim. 4:1
"Easy-believism"
Error—2 Tim. 2:17–18; 1 John 4:6

False doctrines—2 Tim. 4:3
Hate—1 Peter 2:1
Lack of discernment—Eph. 5:6
Lies—1 Tim. 4:2
New Age beliefs
Pride/Haughtiness—Ps. 36:2–3
Unsubmissive—2 Tim. 3:2
Unteachable—1 Tim. 6:20–21;
2 Tim. 3:7

BIND	LOOSE
▸ Spirit of Error—1 John 4:6	▸ Spirit of Truth—John 14:17; 15:26; John 16:13 ▸ Spirit of Promise—Eph. 1:13; Gal. 3:14

SPIRIT OF FEAR

Abandonment—Prov. 19:7
Abuse—Judg. 19:25
Accusations—Ps. 31:18

Agitation
Anxiety—1 Peter 5:7
Apprehension

Cannot call upon God
Careful, unduly
Cautious, unduly
Compromise
Condemnation
Confusion—Jer. 3:25; James 3:16
Crying, continual—Matt. 15:23
Daydreaming
Depression—Ps. 42:5; Lam. 3:19–20
Distrust
Doubt—Matt. 8:26; Rev. 21:8
Doubting assurance of salvation
Dread—Ps. 119:39
Embarrassment—Ezra 9:6
Escapism—2 Cor. 10:4–5
Excitable, overly
Faithlessness—Prov. 14:4
Fantasy**—Gen. 6:5
Fear of:
   Accusation
   Authority
   Closed-in places
   Condemnation
   Confrontation—Matt. 10:28
   Correction
   Danger—Prov. 16:4
   Darkness—Is. 59:9–10
   Death—Ps. 55:4; Heb. 2:14–15
   Disapproval
   Failure—Gen. 42:28
   Germs
   Giving/receiving love
   God (in an unhealthy way)
   Heights
   Judgment
   Losing salvation
   Man—Prov. 29:25

   Touching
Frustration
Hormonal imbalance
Headaches***
Heart attacks—Lev. 26:36; Ps. 55:4;
   Luke 21:26; John 14:1
High blood pressure
Hypochondria
Hysteria
Inadequacy
Indecision
Indifference
Ineptness
Inferiority complex
Insanity—Matt. 17:15
Insecurity
Insomnia
Intimidation
Isolation
Jealousy—Num. 5:14; Songs 8:6
Judgmentalism
Lack of trust
Loneliness—Job 28:4
Low self-esteem
Mind control
Moodiness
Nightmares—Ps. 91:5–6
Negativity
No fellowship with the Father
Orphaned—Jer. 47:3
Panic
Paralysis
Paranoia
Passivity
Phobias—Is. 13:7–8; 2 Tim. 1:7
Playacting
Pouting
Pretension

Procrastination—Prov. 6:6
Recluse
Resentment
Restlessness
Roving
Schizophrenia—Deut. 28:28
Self-awareness, hyper- or excessive
Self-rejection
Self-reward
Sensitivity, hyper- or excessive
Sickness—2 Kings 20:1
Skepticism—2 Peter 3:3
Sleepiness—1 Thess. 5:6–7
Sleeplessness—Prov. 4:16
Sophistication
Sorrow—Ps. 13:2; 116:3
Spiritual blindness—Isa. 56:10;
   Hos. 9:7

Stress
Stuttering—Isa. 32:4
Suspicion
Teeth-grinding—Ps. 112:10
Tension
Terror—Job 31:23
Theatrics
Timidity—2 Tim. 1:7
Torment—Ps. 55:5; 1 John 4:18
Trembling—Job 4:14; Ps. 55:5
Trust, lack of
Unbelief—Matt. 13:58; Heb. 4:11
Unreality
Unworthiness
Vexation—Eccl. 1:14
Worry—Matt. 6:25–28

Notes:
** For Fantasy, also see Spirit of Whoredom
*** For Headaches, also see Spirit of Infirmity
****For Resentment, also see Spirit of Jealousy

BIND	LOOSE
▸ Spirit of Fear—2 Tim. 1:7; Ps. 55:5	▸ Peace—1 Thess. 5:23; Gal. 5:22; Eph. 4:3 ▸ Joy—Ps. 5:11, 51:12; Gal. 5:22–23

SPIRIT OF HEAVINESS

Abandonment
Bastard (to alienate)—Deut. 23:2;
   Zech. 9:6
Broken-hearted—Ps. 69:20; Prov.
   12:18; 15:3, 13; 18:14; Luke 4:18
Burdened
Condemnation—2 Cor. 3:9
Continual sadness—Prov. 15:13;
   Neh. 2:2
Critical
Cruel—Prov. 6:34
Crying—Matt. 15:23
Death—Job 3:5; Isa. 8:19
Defeatism—Prov. 7:26–27
Despair—Job 7:15; 2 Cor. 1:8–9
Despondency—Isa. 61:3
Dejection—2 Cor. 1:8–9
Discouragement
Disgust
Disorder
Dread—Deut. 1:29
Drivenness, excessive
Escape
False burden
False guilt
Fatigue
Gloom
Gluttony
Grief—Job 6:2; Ps. 31:9
Guilt
Headache
Heartbreak, heartache
Hopelessness—2 Cor. 1:8–9
Hurt

Hyperactivity
Indifference
Inner hurts
Insomnia—Neh. 2:2
Introspection
Laziness—Prov. 19:15
Lethargy
Listlessness
Loneliness
Morbidity
Mourning, excessive—Luke 4:18;
   Isa. 6:13
Pain—Jer. 6:24; 15:18; Luke 9:39
Passivity—Prov. 10:4
Poverty—Prov. 13:18
Pressure
Rejection
Restlessness—John 14:1
Self-pity—Ps. 69:20
Shame—Ps. 44:15; Eph. 5:12
Sleepiness
Sorrow—Prov. 15:13; Isa. 65:14
Suicide—Ps. 18:5
Tiredness—Isa. 40:30; 57:10
Torment—Ps. 22:16; 1 John 4:18
Troubled spirit—Luke 4:18; Prov.
   18:14; 26:22
Unworthiness
Vagabond—Gen. 4:12, 14; Acts
   19:13
Wanderer—Jude 1:13
Weariness—Ps. 109:22
Wounded spirit—Prov. 15:4; 1 Cor.
   8:12

BIND	LOOSE
▸ Spirit of Heaviness—Isa. 61:3; Ps. 69:20; Prov. 12:25	▸ Comforter—Heb. 13:15 ▸ Praise—Ps. 22:22; 42:11 ▸ Joy—Isa. 61:5; Neh. 12:43; Job 41:22

SPIRIT OF INFIRMITY

ADD—Matt. 8:16–17

ADHD—Mark 7:32

Allergies

Arthritis—Deut. 28:35; Prov. 14:30; John 5:4

Asthma—John 5:4; Prov. 16:24

Bent body or spine—Luke 13:11

Bitterness—Deut. 28:20; 1 Sam. 5:6; Job 7:11

Bleeding—Matt. 9:20

Blindness—Gen. 48:10; Lev. 26:16; Deut. 28:28; Luke 7:21

Bronchitis

Cancer—Luke 13:11; John 5:4

Chronic diseases—Job 33:19–25; Ps. 102:5

Chronic fatigue syndrome

Colds

Deafness

Death—Ps. 102:11

Diseases—Lev. 26:16

Disorders

Epilepsy—1 Sam. 21:15

Fainting—Lam. 1:13

Feebleness—Prov. 16:24

Fever—Matt. 8:15

Fungus infections—Luke 5:12

Generational curses—Ex. 20:5; Lev. 26:39; Num. 14:18; Deut. 5:9

Hallucinations—Deut. 28:20

Hatred—Deut. 28:22

Hay fever

Headaches or Migraines

Heart attack—Lev. 26:36; Ps. 102:4

Impotence—Acts 3:2; 4:9

Infections—Deut. 28:22

Inflammation—2 Chron. 21:15

Insanity—Deut. 28:28–29

Lameness—Acts 3:2; 4:9

Lunatic—Zech. 12:4

Madness—Prov. 17:22

Mania—Prov. 26:21

Mental illness—Matt. 17:15; Mark 5:5

Oppression**—Acts 10:38

Paralysis (Palsy)—Ps. 102:5; Prov. 15:20; Matt. 4:24

Paranoia—Deut. 28:67

Physical disorders or trauma, lingering—Luke 13:11

Plague (curse)—Luke 7:21

Poverty—Deut. 28: 20–33, 38
Schizophrenia—Deut. 28:28–29
Seizures
Senility
Skin disorders—Deut. 28:27
Slavery
Spirit of death—Deut. 28:53
Torment—Matt. 4:24; Luke 16:28

Turret's Syndrome
Ulcers—Deut. 28:27; Luke 16:20
Unforgiveness
Venereal Disease—Ps. 38
Weakness, chronic—Luke 13:11;
John 5:5
Wounded spirit—Lev. 26:16; Prov.
18:14

Note:
**For Oppression, also see Spirit of Heaviness

BIND	LOOSE
▸ Spirit of Infirmity—Luke 13:11; Prov. 18:14	▸ Wholeness—Matt. 6:22; 9:22 ▸ Health—3 John 1:2; Jer. 33:6

SPIRIT OF JEALOUSY

Accusations—1 Tim. 5:19
Anger—Gen. 4:5–6; Prov. 6:34;
14:29; 22:24–25; 29:22–23
Argumentative
Backbiting—Prov. 19:5
Belittling
Bickering—1 Tim. 6:4
Bitterness—Prov. 18:19
Blasphemy
Burn—Ps. 79:5
Causing divisions
Coarse jesting (inappropriate/dis-
honorable words)—Eph. 5:4
Competitive, excessively—Gen.
4:4–5
Contentious—Prov. 13:10

Covetousness—1 Tim. 6:10
Critical
Cruelty—Prov. 27:4; Songs 8:6
Cry, inability to
Cursing—Prov 18:21
Debates, seeking to cause
Deception—1 Tim. 6:5
Destruction—Job 26:6
Discontent—1 Tim. 5:13
Disputes—Job 23:7
Dissatisfaction
Distrust
Divisions, causing—Gal. 5:19
Dreamer
Enmity—Rom. 8:7
Envy—Gen. 21:9

Factiousness
Faultfinding
Fighting—Ps. 56:1
Gangs
Gossip
Greed—Prov. 15:27
Hardness of heart—James 1:14;
1 Tim. 4:1
Hatred—Gen. 3; 7:3–4, 8; 1 Thess.
4:8
Hurt
Indifference
Inferiority
Insecurity
Judging
Lying—1 Tim. 4:1; Prov. 12:22
Malice—Prov. 4:16–17
Materialism—Ps. 30:6
Mocking—Jer. 15:17–18
Murder—Gen. 4:8
Quarrelling—Col. 3:13

Rage—Prov. 6:34
Rebellion—Deut. 21:18
Restlessness
Retaliation
Revenge—Prov. 6:34; 14:16–17
Sadism
Self-centeredness—Luke 18:11
Self-hatred
Selfishness—2 Peter 2:10
Slander—Prov. 10:18
Spite—Prov. 6:34; 14:16–17
Stealing
Strife—Prov. 10:12
Suicide—Acts 1:18
Suspicion
Temper—Prov. 6:34
Unforgiveness
Unworthiness
Violence—Prov. 16:29
Wickedness—Prov. 3: 31

BIND	LOOSE
▶ Spirit of Jealousy—Num. 5:14, 30; Ezek. 8:3	▶ Love—1 Peter 1:22; Gal. 5:22; Prov. 10:12

SPIRIT OF PERVERSION / WHOREDOM

Abortion
Adultery—Ezra 16:15, 28; Prov.
5:1–14
Adulterous fantasy—Prov. 12:26
Arrogance—Rom. 1:29–31
Atheism—Prov. 14:2; Rom. 1:30

Bastard (unholy covenant)—Deut.
23:2; Zech. 9:6
Bisexuality
Child abuse
Confusion (spirit of Egypt)—Isa.
19:3

Contentious—Rom. 1:29; Phil.
2:14–16; 1 Tim. 6:4–5; Titus
3:10–11
Crankiness
Cruelty—Ps. 74:20
Deception—Prov. 28:18; Rom.
1:30–31
Dissatisfaction, chronic
Diviner—Hosea 4:12
Dizziness—Isa. 19:14
Doctrinal error (twisting the Word)
Doubt—Deut. 28:66
Drunkard—Prov. 23:21
Emotional dissatisfaction
Emotional weakness
Excessive activity
Exhibitionism
Evil actions—Prov. 17:20, 23
False teachings—Mark 13:22;
2 Tim. 3:13; Deut. 13:6–8
Fantasies (lustful)
Filthy-mindedness—Prov. 2:12;
23:33
Foolishness—Prov. 1:22; 19:1
Fornication—Hosea 4:13–19; Rom.
1:29; Heb. 13:14
Frigidity
Greed—Prov. 22:22
Guilt
Harlotry—Prov. 23:27–28
Hatred—Ps. 139:22; Prov. 26:26
Hoarding
Homosexuality—Gen. 19:4–7;
Rom. 1:27
Idolatry—Jude 2:17; Hosea 4:12;
Ezra 16
Illegitimate children—Gen. 19:36–
38

Incest—Gen. 19:31–33
Incubus and Succubus—Gen. 6:2–4
Lesbianism—Rom. 1:26
Love of power—Job 2:6; Ps. 10:15;
Lam. 5:8
Lust for:
Authority
Body (sexual)
Food
Money—Prov. 15:27; 1 Tim.
6:7–14
Position
Perverse sexual acts
Power
Sex
Social standing
The world
Worldliness
Lust (all kinds)—Prov. 23:31–35
Marking, cutting, or tattoos—Lev.
19:28
Masturbation
Pedophilia—Lev. 19:29
Pornography
Poverty—Lev. 26:18–20
Prostitution (of spirit, soul, or
body)—Prov. 5:1–14; 22:14
Rape—2 Sam. 13:1–14
Sadomasochism
Seduction—1 Tim. 4:1; 2 Tim.
3:13; Prov. 1:10
Self-exposure
Self-gratification—Prov. 5:3–6
Self, lover of—Prov. 4:24
Sensuality—Jude 1:19
Sexual deviation—Gen. 19:8
Sexual dissatisfaction—Ezra 16:28

Sexual perversion—Rom. 1:17–32; 2 Tim. 3:2
Sexual sin, all—Jude 1:7–8
Shame—Ps. 44:15
Stubbornness
Sodomy—Gen. 19:5; Jude 1:7
Transvestite
Unbelief—Matt. 13:58
Uncontrollable sexual desires— 1 Cor. 6:13–16; Phil. 3:19

Unfaithfulness—Prov. 5:1–14; Ezra 16:15, 28
Weakness—Gen. 38:15–18
Whoredom—Hos. 3:12–14
Worldliness—James 4:4
Worry, chronic—Prov. 19:3; Job 30:27
Wounded spirit—Prov. 15:4

BIND	LOOSE
▶ Spirit of Perversion—Isa. 19:14; Rom. 1:17–32 ▶ Spirit of Whoredom—Lev. 19:29; Ezek. 16:28–29; Isa. 19:14; Hosea 4:12; 5:4; Jer. 3:9	▶ Chastity—1 Peter 3:2; 2 Cor. 11:2 ▶ Discernment—Job 6:30; Ezek. 44:23; Heb. 5:14 ▶ Godliness—1 Tim. 4:8; 2 Peter 3:11 ▶ Purity—1 Tim. 4:12

SPIRIT OF SLUMBER / UNBELIEF

ADD
ADHD
Blasphemer—2 Tim. 3:2
Blind—Rom. 2:19–20
Can't hear the Word of God
Can't stay awake in church—Rom. 13:11–12
Confusion—Job 10:15
Distracted easily—Ps. 88:15
Dizziness—James 3:16
Fear—1 John 4:18
Lazy—Prov. 19:15

Lethargy
Mental slowness
Perversions
Sickness:**
  Anemia
  Arthritis—Prov. 12:4; 14:30
  Asthma
  Circulation problems
  Chronic Fatigue Syndrome
  Eye disorders—Rev. 3:18
  Hearing problems (dull of hearing)—Matt. 13:13–14

Palpatations

Sleepiness—Job 33:15

Sleeplessness—Prov. 4:16

Terror—Job 31:23

Torment—1 John 4:18

Unbelief—Heb. 3:12

Notes:

**For sickness, also see Spirit of Infirmity

BIND	LOOSE
▸ Spirit of Unbelief, Stupor, or Slumber—Rom. 11:8; Isa. 6:9; Matt. 13:14	▸ Being filled with the Spirit—Acts 2:4; Eph. 5:18 ▸ Opened eyes—John 9:30; Ps. 119:18

BREAKING UNHOLY SOUL-TIES

With your eyes open:

> *In the name of Jesus Christ, and by the authority I have in Him, I cut any and all ungodly soul-ties with past partners or husband/ wife [name them] that have been abusive, unholy, or illicit. And I sever physical and spiritual ties with _____[name also anyone else with whom you have been intimate]. I renounce and break all sexual relationships that were in disobedience to God. I command all strongmen and their demonic households be plundered and destroyed. I bind, renounce, and remove any evil predator spirits that have reinforced those soul-ties or those transferred to me through evil associations.*
>
> *Devils, you have no more access to my body, soul, or spirit through those ties, and the doorway is shut and sealed by the blood of the Lamb!*
>
> *I also declare by the authority of Jesus Christ that neither do you, demonic powers, have any power over my family. All access to any family members or their children through soul-ties is hereby cut.*

I pray, Lord Jesus, that the Holy Spirit will rebuild godly relationships and covenant ties in my life according to your perfect will. I call for the full power of the cross, the blood, the resurrection, and the ascension against Satan's plans and schemes for my family and for me. Thank you for hearing my proclamation and prayer, in your name, Amen.*

*Adapted by permission from Kanaan Bedieninge, *Prayers of Renunciation* (Cape Town, South Africa: np., nd.), 87.

RENOUNCING FREEMASONRY

FREEMASONRY ROOTS MAY CAUSE ...

- spiritual confusion among leadership;
- division among clergy and eldership;
- the "Lewis curse": affects the firstborn male (work/finances/family/marriage/health/stature/position);
- illness or marriage breakup among Christian leaders and their families;
- "death" of churches in renewal;
- retardation of evangelism (stifles outreach, fellowship, vision, relationship);
- the church's failure to enter into fresh vision and ministry (retaining "tradition");
- businesses to have lack of growth and final breakthrough among Christian employers;
- favoritism among certain members of legal, judicial, police, architectural professions;
- attempts to combine religious and philosophical thinking;
- a freemasonic-founded community to be distant from the church (but open to cults);

- cyclical problems to return to individuals, families, schools, businesses, churches, government, and politics.

PRAYER OF RELEASE FOR FREEMASONS AND THEIR DESCENDANTS

If you were once a Mason or are a descendant of a Mason, we recommend that you pray through the following prayer *from your heart*. Don't be like the Masons who are given their obligations and oaths one line at a time, without prior knowledge of the requirements. Read it through first so you know what's involved. It is best to pray this aloud with a Christian witness or counselor present. We suggest a brief pause following each paragraph to allow the Holy Spirit to show any additional issues that require attention.

Father God, creator of heaven and earth, I come to you in the name of Jesus Christ, your Son. I come as a sinner seeking forgiveness and cleansing from all sins committed against you, and others made in your image. I honor my earthly father and mother and all of my ancestors of flesh and blood, and of the spirit by adoption, and godparents, but I utterly turn away from and renounce all their sins. I forgive all my ancestors for the effects of their sins on my children and on me. I confess and renounce all of my own sins. I renounce and rebuke Satan and every spiritual power of his affecting my family and me.

In the name of the Lord Jesus Christ, I renounce and forsake all involvement in Freemasonry or any other lodge or craft by my ancestors and myself. I renounce and cut off witchcraft, the principal spirit behind Freemasonry, and I renounce Baphomet, the spirits of antichrist, death, and deception, and the curse of the Luciferian doctrine. I renounce the idolatry, blasphemy, secrecy and deception of Masonry at every level. I specifically renounce the insecurity, the love of position and power, the love of money, the avarice or greed, and the pride that would have led my ancestors into Masonry. I renounce all fears that held them in Masonry, especially the fears of death, fears of men, and fears of trusting.

I also renounce and break the code of silence enforced by Freemasonry and

*the occult on my family and myself. I renounce and repent of all pride and arro-
gance, which opened the door for the slavery and bondage of Freemasonry to
afflict my family and me. I now shut every door of witchcraft and deception
operating in my life and seal it closed with the blood of Christ. I renounce every
covenant, every blood covenant, and every alliance with Freemasonry or the
spiritual powers behind it made by my family or by me.*

*I renounce every position held in the lodge by any of my ancestors, including
"Tyler," "Master," "Worshipful Master," or any other. I renounce the calling of
any man "Master," for Jesus Christ is my only Master and Lord, and He forbids
anyone else having that title. I renounce the entrapping of others into Masonry
and observing the helplessness of others during the rituals.*

*I renounce the effects of Masonry passed on to me through any female ances-
tor who felt distrusted and rejected by her husband as he entered and attended
any lodge and refused to tell her of his secret activities. I also renounce all obligations, oaths, and curses enacted by every female member of my family through
any direct membership of all Women's Orders of Freemasonry, the Order of the
Eastern Star, or any other Masonic or occult organization.*

FIRST DEGREE (BLUE LODGE)

*In the name of Jesus Christ, I renounce the oaths taken and the
curses and iniquities involved in the First or Entered Apprentice
Degree, especially their effects on the throat and tongue. I renounce the
Hoodwink blindfold and its effects on spirit, emotions, and eyes, including all confusion, fear of the dark, fear of the light, and fear of sudden
noises. I renounce the blinding of spiritual truth, the darkness of the
soul, false imaginations, condescension, and the spirit of poverty caused
by the ritual of this degree. I also renounce the usurping of the marriage
covenant by the removal of the wedding ring. I renounce the secret
word, BOAZ, and its Masonic meaning. I renounce the serpent clasp on
the apron, and the spirit of Python, which it brought to squeeze the
spiritual life out of me.*

*I renounce the ancient pagan teaching from Babylon and Egypt,
and the symbolism of the First Tracing Board. I renounce the mixing*

and mingling of truth and error, the mythology, fabrications, and lies taught as truth, and the dishonesty by leaders as to the true understanding of the ritual. I renounce the presentation to every compass direction, for all the Earth is the Lord's, and everything in it.

I renounce the cable tow noose around the neck, the fear of choking, and also every spirit causing asthma, hay fever, emphysema, or any other breathing difficulty. I renounce the ritual dagger, or the compass point, sword, or spear held against the breast, the fear of death by stabbing, pain, and the fear of heart attack from this degree, and the absolute secrecy demanded under a witchcraft oath and sealed by kissing the Volume of the Sacred Law. I also renounce kneeling to the false deity known as the Great Architect of the Universe, and humbly ask the One True God to forgive me for this idolatry.

I renounce the pride of proven character and good standing required prior to joining Freemasonry, and the resulting self-righteousness of being good enough to stand before God without the need of a savior. I now pray for healing of (throat, vocal cords, nasal passages, sinus, bronchial tubes, etc.) for healing of the speech area, and the release of the Word of God to me and through my family and me.

SECOND DEGREE (CRAFT LODGE)

In the name of Jesus Christ I renounce the oaths taken and the curses and iniquities involved in the Second or Fellow Craft Degree of Masonry, especially the curses on the heart and chest. I renounce the secret words SHIBBOLETH and JACHIN and all their Masonic meaning. I renounce the ancient pagan teaching and symbolism of the Second Tracing Board. I renounce the Sign of Reverence to the Generative Principle.

I cut off emotional hardness, apathy, indifference, unbelief, and deep anger from my family and me. In the name of Jesus Christ I pray for the healing of (the chest/lung/heart area) and also for the healing of my emotions, and ask to be made sensitive to the Holy Spirit of God.

THIRD DEGREE (ANCIENT CRAFT LODGE)

I renounce the oaths taken and the curses involved in the Third or Master Mason degree, especially the curses on the stomach and the womb area. I renounce the secret words MAHA BONE, MACHABEN, MACHBINNA, and TUBAL CAIN, and all their Masonic meaning. I renounce the ancient pagan teaching and symbolism of the Third Tracing Board used in the ritual. I renounce the Spirit of Death from the blows to the head enacted as ritual murder, the fear of death, false martyrdom, fear of violent gang attack, assault, or rape, and the help-lessness of this degree. I renounce the falling into the coffin or stretcher involved in the ritual of murder.

I renounce the false resurrection of this degree, because only Jesus Christ is the Resurrection and the Life! I also renounce the blasphemous kissing of the Bible on a witchcraft oath. I cut off all spirits of death, witchcraft, and deception in the name of Jesus. I pray for the healing of (the stomach, gall bladder, womb, liver, and any other organs of my body affected by Masonry), and I ask for a release of compassion and understanding for my family and me.

HOLY ROYAL ARCH DEGREE

I renounce and forsake the oaths taken and the curses involved in the Holy Royal Arch Degree of Masonry, especially the oath regarding the removal of the head from the body and the exposing of the brains to the hot sun. I renounce the Mark Lodge and the mark in the form of squares and angles that marks the person for life. I also reject the jewel or talisman that may have been made from this mark sign and worn at lodge meetings. I renounce the false secret name of God, JAHBULON, and declare total rejection of all worship of the false pagan gods, Bul or Baal, and On or Osiris. I also renounce the password AMMI RUHA-MAH and all its Masonic meaning. I renounce the false communion or Eucharist taken in this degree, all the mockery, skepticism, and unbelief about the redemptive work of Jesus Christ on the cross of Calvary. I cut off these curses and their effects on my family and me in the name of Jesus Christ. I pray for healing (of the brain, the mind, etc.).

EIGHTEENTH DEGREE

I renounce the oaths taken and the curses, iniquities, and penalties involved in the Eighteenth Degree of Masonry, the Most Wise Sovereign Knight of the Pelican and the Eagle and Sovereign Prince Rose Croix of Heredom. I renounce and reject the Pelican witchcraft spirit, as well as the occult influence of the Rosicrucians and the Kabbala in this degree.

I renounce the claim that the death of Jesus Christ was a "dire calamity," and also the deliberate mockery and twisting of the Christian doctrine of the atonement. I renounce the blasphemy and rejection of the deity of Jesus Christ and the secret words IGNE NATURA RENOVATUR INTEGRA and its burning. I renounce the mockery of the communion taken in this degree, including the biscuit, salt, and white wine.

THIRTIETH DEGREE

I renounce the oaths taken and the curses and iniquities involved in the Thirtieth Degree of Masonry, the Grand Knight Kadosh and Knight of the Black and White Eagle. I renounce the secret passwords STIBIUM ALKABAR and PHARASH-KOH and all they mean.

THIRTY-FIRST DEGREE

I renounce the oaths taken and the curses involved in the Thirty-First Degree of Masonry and the Grand Inspector Inquisitor Commander. I renounce all the gods and goddesses of Egypt that are honored in this degree, including Anubis and the ram's head, Osiris the sun god, Isis the sister and wife of Osiris, and also the moon goddess. I renounce the Soul of Cheres, the false symbol of immortality, the chamber of the dead, and the false teaching of reincarnation.

THIRTY-SECOND DEGREE

I renounce the oaths taken and the curses and iniquities involved in the Thirty-Second Degree of Masonry, the Sublime Prince of the Royal Secret. I renounce the secret passwords PHAAL/PHARASH-KOL and all they mean. I renounce Masonry's false trinitarian deity AUM and its parts, Brahma the creator, Vishnu the preserver, and Shiva the destroyer. I renounce the deity of AHURA-MAZDA, the claimed spirit or source of all light, and the worship with fire, which is an abomination to God, and also the drinking from a human skull in many rites.

YORK RITES

I renounce and forsake the oaths taken and the curses and iniquities involved in the York Rite Degrees of Freemasonry. I renounce the Mark Lodge and the mark in the form of squares and angles, which marks the person for life. I also reject the jewel or occult talisman which may have been made from this mark sign and worn at lodge meetings, the Mark Master Degree with its secret word JOPPA, and its penalty of having the right ear smote off and the curse of permanent deafness, as well as the right hand being chopped off for being an imposter.

I also renounce and forsake the oaths taken and the curses and iniquities involved in the other York Rite Degrees, including Past Master, with the penalty of having my tongue split from tip to root, and of the Most Excellent Master Degree, in which the penalty is to have my breast torn open and my heart and vital organs removed and exposed to rot on the dung hill.

I renounce and forsake the oaths taken and the curses and iniquities involved in the Royal Master Degree of the York Rite; the Select Master Degree with its penalty to have my hands chopped off to the stumps, to have my eyes plucked out from their sockets, and to have my body quartered and thrown among the rubbish of the Temple.

I renounce and forsake the oaths taken and the curses and iniquities involved in the Super Excellent Master Degree along with the penalty of having my thumbs cut off, my eyes put out, my body bound in fetters and brass, and conveyed captive to a strange land; and also of the Knights Order of the Red Cross, along with the penalty of having my house torn down and being hanged on the exposed timbers.

*I renounce the Knights Templar Degree and the secret words of
KEB RAIOTH/KEPRAIOTH and also the Knights of Malta Degree
and the secret words MAHER-SHALAL-HASH-BAZ.*

*I renounce the vows taken on a human skull, the crossed swords, and
the curse and death wish of Judas of having the head cut off and placed
on top of a church spire. I renounce the unholy communion and especially
of drinking from a human skull in many rites.*

THIRTY-THIRD (SUPREME) DEGREE

*In the name of Jesus Christ I renounce the oaths taken and the curses
and iniquities involved in the supreme Thirty-Third Degree of Freemasonry, the Grand Sovereign Inspector General. I renounce the secret
passwords, DEMOLAY-HIRUM ABIFF, FREDERICK OF PRUS-
SIA, MICHA, MACHA, BEALIM, and ADONAI, and all their
occult and Masonic meanings. I renounce all of the obligations of every
Masonic degree and all penalties invoked. I renounce and utterly forsake
The Great Architect of the Universe, who is revealed in this degree as
Lucifer, and his false claim to be the universal fatherhood of God. I
renounce the cable tow around the neck. I renounce the death wish that
the wine drunk from a human skull should turn to poison and the skele-
ton whose cold arms are invited if the oath of this degree is violated. I
renounce the three infamous assassins of their grand master: law, property, and religion, and the greed and witchcraft involved in the attempt
to manipulate and control the rest of mankind.*

*In the name of God the Father, Jesus Christ the Son, and the Holy
Spirit, I renounce and break the curses and iniquities involved in the
idolatry, blasphemy, secrecy, and deception of Freemasonry at every
level, and I appropriate the blood of Jesus Christ to cleanse all the consequences of these from my life. I now revoke all previous consent given by
any of my ancestors or myself to be deceived.*

ALL OTHER DEGREES

There are differences between British Commonwealth Masonry and
American and Prince Hall Masonry in the higher degrees (only the

Eighteenth, Thirtieth, Thirty-first, Thirty-second, and Thirty-third Degrees are operated in British Commonwealth countries). Degrees unique to Americans are marked with three stars (***) at paragraph's beginning.

I renounce all the other oaths taken, the rituals of every other degree and the curses involved. I renounce all other lodges and secret societies, such as Prince Hall Freemasonry, Mormonism, the Order of Amaranth, Oddfellows, Buffalos, Druids, Foresters, Orange, Elks, Moose, and Eagles Lodges, the Ku Klux Klan, the Grange, the Woodmen of the World, Riders of the Red Robe, the Knights of Pythias, the Mystic Order of the Veiled Prophets of the Enchanted Realm, the women's Orders of the Eastern Star and of the White Shrine of Jerusalem, the girls' order of the Daughters of the Eastern Star, the International Orders of Job's Daughters, and the Rainbow, and the boys' Order of DeMolay and their effects on me and all my family.

SHRINERS

**** *I renounce the oaths taken and the curses, iniquities, and penalties involved in the Ancient Arabic Order of the Nobles of the Mystic Shrine. I renounce the piercing of the eyeballs with a three-edged blade, the flaying of the feet, the madness, and the worship of the false god Allah as the god of our fathers. I renounce the hoodwink, the mock hanging, the mock beheading, the mock drinking of the blood of the victim, the mock dog urinating on the initiate, and the offering of urine as a commemoration.*

**** *I renounce the oaths taken and the curses, iniquities, and penalties involved in the American and Grand Orient Lodges, including of the Secret Master Degree, its secret password of ADONAI, and its Masonic and occult meaning;*

**** *of the Perfect Master Degree, its secret password of MAH-HAH-BONE, and its penalty of being smitten to the Earth with a setting maul;*

**** *of the Intimate Secretary Degree, its secret password of JEHOVAH* *used blasphemously, and its penalties of having my body dissected and of having my vital organs cut into pieces and thrown to the beasts of the field;*

*** *of the Provost and Judge Degree, its secret password of HIRUM-TITO-CIVI-KY, and the penalty of having my nose cut off;*

*** *of the Intendant of the Building Degree, of its secret password AKAR-JAI-JAH, and the penalty of having my eyes put out, my body cut in two and exposing my bowels;*

*** *of the Elected Knights of the Nine Degree, its secret password NEKAM NAKAH, and its penalty of having my head cut off and stuck on the highest pole in the East;*

*** *of the Illustrious Elect of Fifteen Degree, with its secret password ELIGNAM, and its penalties of having my body opened perpendicularly and horizontally, the entrails exposed to the air for eight hours so that flies may prey on them, and for my head to be cut off and placed on a high pinnacle;*

*** *of the Sublime Knights elect of the Twelve Degree, its secret password STOLKIN-ADONAI, and its penalty of having my hand cut in twain;*

*** *of the Grand Master Architect Degree, its secret password RAB-BANAIM, and its penalties;*

*** *of the Knight of the Ninth Arch of Solomon Degree, its secret password JEHOVAH, and its penalty of having my body given to the beasts of the forest as prey;*

*** *of the Grand Elect, Perfect and Sublime Mason Degree, its secret password, and its penalty of having my body cut open and my bowels given to vultures for food;*

COUNCIL OF PRINCES OF JERUSALEM

*** *of the Knights of the East Degree, its secret password RAPH-O-DOM, and its penalties;*

*** *of the Prince of Jerusalem Degree, its secret password TEBET-ADAR, and its penalty of being stripped naked and having my heart pierced with a ritual dagger;*

CHAPTER OF THE ROSE CROIX

*** *of the Knight of the East and West Degree, its secret password ABADDON, and its penalty of incurring the severe wrath of the Almighty Creator of Heaven and Earth;*

COUNCIL OF KADOSH

*** *I renounce the oaths taken and the curses, iniquities, and penalties involved in the Grand Pontiff Degree, its secret password EMMANUEL, and its penalties;*

*** *of the Grand Master of Symbolic Lodges Degree, its secret passwords JEKSON and STOLKIN, and the penalties;*

*** *of the Noachite of Prussian Knight Degree, its secret password PELEG, and its penalties;*

*** *of the Knight of the Royal Axe Degree, its secret password NOAH-BEZALEEL-SODONIAS, and its penalties;*

*** *of the Chief of the Tabernacle Degree, its secret password URIEL-JEHOVAH, and its penalty that I agree the Earth should open up and engulf me up to my neck so I perish;*

*** *of the Prince of the Tabernacle Degree, and its penalty that I should be stoned to death and my body left above ground to rot;*

*** *of the Knight of the Brazen Serpent Degree, its secret password MOSES-JOHANNES, and its penalty that I have my heart eaten by venomous serpents;*

*** *of the Prince of Mercy Degree, its secret password GOMEL, JEHOVAH-JACHIN, and its penalty of condemnation and spite by the entire universe;*

*** *of the Knight Commander of the Temple Degree, its secret password SOLOMON, and its penalty of receiving the severest wrath of Almighty God inflicted upon me;*

*** *of the Knight Commander of the Sun, or Prince Adept Degree, its secret password STIBIUM, and its penalties of having my tongue thrust through with a red-hot iron, of my eyes being plucked out, of my senses of smelling and hearing being removed, of having my hands cut off and in that condition to be left for voracious animals to devour me, or executed by lightning from heaven;*

*** *of the Grand Scottish Knight of Saint Andrew Degree, its secret password NEKAMAH-FURLAC, and its penalties;*

*** *of the Council of Kadosh Grand Pontiff Degree, its secret password EMMANUEL, and its penalties.*

I renounce the ancient pagan teaching and symbolism of the First Tracing Board, the Second Tracing Board, and the Third Tracing Board used in the ritual of the Blue Lodge. I renounce the pagan ritual of the "Point Within a Circle" with all its bondages and phallus worship. I renounce the occult mysticism of the black and white mosaic-chequered floor with the tressellated border and five-pointed blazing star. I renounce the symbol "G" and its veiled pagan symbolism and bondages. I renounce and utterly forsake The Great Architect of the Universe, who is revealed in the higher degrees as Lucifer, and his false claim to be the universal fatherhood of God. I also renounce the false claim that Lucifer is the Morning Star and Shining One, and I declare that Jesus Christ is the Bright and Morning Star of Revelation 22:16.

I renounce the All-Seeing Third Eye of Freemasonry, or Horus, in the forehead and its pagan and occult symbolism. I now close that Third Eye and all occult ability to see into the spiritual realm, in the name of the Lord Jesus Christ, and put my trust in the Holy Spirit sent by Jesus Christ for all I need to know on spiritual matters. I renounce all false communions taken, all mockery of the redemptive work of Jesus Christ on the cross of Calvary, all unbelief, confusion (spirit of dizziness), and depression (spirit of heaviness), and all worship of Lucifer as God. I renounce and forsake the lie of Freemasonry that man is not sinful, but merely imperfect, and so can redeem himself through good works. I rejoice that the Bible states that I cannot do a single thing to earn my salvation, but that I can only be saved by grace through faith in Jesus Christ and what He accomplished on the cross of Calvary.

In the name of Jesus Christ I renounce Hiram Abiff, the false savior of Freemasons. I renounce the false resurrection, because only Jesus Christ is the Resurrection and the Life!

I renounce all fear of insanity, anguish, death wishes, suicide, and death in the name of Jesus Christ. Jesus Christ conquered death, and He alone holds the keys of death and hell, and I rejoice that He holds my life in His hands now. He came to give me life abundantly and eternally, and I believe His promises.

I renounce all anger, hatred, murderous thoughts, revenge, retaliation, spiritual apathy, false religion, and all unbelief, especially unbelief in the Holy Bible and God's Word, and all compromise of God's Word. I renounce all spiritual searching into false religions and all striving to please God. I rest in the knowledge that I have found my Lord and Savior Jesus Christ, and that He has found me.

I will burn all objects in my possession that connect me with all lodges and occult organizations, including Masonry, Witchcraft, and Mormonism, and all regalia, aprons, books of rituals, certificates, awards, rings, and other jewelry. I renounce the effects these or other objects of Masonry, such as the compass, the square, the noose, or the blindfold, have on my family or me, in Jesus' name.

All participants should now be invited to sincerely carry out the following:

1. *Symbolically remove the blindfold (hoodwink) and give it to the Lord for disposal;*
2. *In the same way, symbolically remove the veil of mourning;*
3. *Symbolically cut and remove the noose from around the neck, gather it up with the cable tow running down the body, and give it all to the Lord for His disposal;*
4. *Renounce the false Freemasonry marriage covenant, removing from*

the fourth finger of the right hand the ring of this false marriage covenant, giving it to the Lord to dispose of it;

5. *Symbolically remove the chains and bondages of Freemasonry from your body;*

6. *Symbolically remove all Freemasonry regalia and armor, especially the apron;*

7. *Repent of and seek forgiveness for having walked on all unholy ground, including Freemasonry lodges and temples, including any Mormon or other occult/Masonic organizations.*

8. *Symbolically remove the ball and chain from the ankles.*

9. *Proclaim that Satan and his demons no longer have any legal rights to mislead and manipulate.*

10. *Repent of unholy soul-ties with other Masons, choosing to stay in covenant with them above family members or fellow Christians.*

Holy Spirit, I ask that you show me anything else I need to do or to pray so that my family and I may be totally free from the consequences of the sins of Masonry, Witchcraft, Mormonism, and Paganism. (Pause, while listening to God, and pray as the Holy Spirit leads.)

Now, dear Father God, I ask humbly for the blood of Jesus Christ, your Son, to cleanse me from all these sins I have confessed and renounced, to cleanse my spirit, my soul, my mind, my emotions, and every part of my body that has been affected by these sins, in Jesus' name!

I also command every cell in my body to come into divine order now, and be healed and made whole. Restore all chemical imbalances and neurological functions, control all cancerous cells, and reverse all degenerative diseases, in the name of the Lord Jesus Christ.

I call on the name of the Lord Jesus to be delivered of all spirits, in accordance with the many promises of the Bible. Deliver me of every spirit of infirmity, all curses, addictions, diseases, or allergies associated with these sins I have confessed and renounced. Lord, baptize me in your Holy Spirit. I take the whole armor of God in accordance with Ephesians 6, and I stand in its protection. Lord Jesus, you are my Lord and my Savior. Thank you for your mercy, your forgiveness, and your love, in the name of Jesus Christ. Amen.*

---

*The material in this appendix is taken by permission from Dr. Selwyn Stevens, "Unmasking Freemasonry—Removing the Hoodwink" (*www.jubilee-resources.com*): P.O. Box 36–044, Wellington 6330, New Zealand (ISBN 1877203–48–3).

RENOUNCING THE ROOTS OF SLAVERY

Dear God, thank you for your throne of grace and mercy because of Jesus Christ's complete work at Calvary. Lord, I ask you to cut me free from every ancestral curse, yoke, false covenant, and iniquity that I inherited. I accept full responsibility for those sins and iniquities, and I repent. Thank you for new freedom.

I confess and forgive the sinful reactions toward those that sold us, those that bought us, those that mistreated and abused us. I forgive and release anger, hatred, denial, bitterness, poverty, rejection, self-rejection, retaliation, murder, violence, curses spoken, and vows sworn to take revenge, in the name of Jesus Christ of Nazareth.

I choose to let sinful emotions and reactions go. I choose to forgive those that were involved in making me a slave, in Jesus' name.

As I receive mercy from you, Lord, I can also extend mercy to those who placed chains on my hands and feet and degraded me (or my family)—whether of my own race or another, in Jesus' name. I forgive them!

I nail everything in detail that was done to my forefathers and to me to the cross of Jesus and cover it with His blood.

I choose to walk away from the pain of the past. I renounce all demonic inheritance and cut free from spirits that may have a hold on me, operating from the countries of my forefathers' origin.

In Jesus' name I renounce all familiar spirits and command you to let me go now!

I renounce and break all demonic roots, tribal markings, all occult callings, ranks, gifts, talents, and abilities now. I break the power of these patterns and cycles over my family and me:

- the fear of hunger
- vagabonds (wanderers)
- all eating disorders
- fatherless generations
- standing with race first, regardless of the truth
- obsessions with food
- denial of truth
- alcoholism and drugs
- all forms of addiction
- inability to handle money
- stealing, gambling, and wasting
- obsession to own land
- all forms of poverty
  - regarding faith
  - about self-worth
  - in relationships
  - with family life
- sexual promiscuity
  - illegitimacy
  - rape
  - abuse
  - all forms of self-comfort

I sever the fruit that has resulted in my life because of the root of slavery, and I command the spirits of bondage, heaviness, fear, jealousy, witchcraft, lies, and all the demons in the household that have been tormenting my family and me for generations. I bind and rebuke you, spirits, in the name of Jesus, and I command you to go now! (Wait for breakthrough.)

Thank you, heavenly Father, that I am your child and that you have adopted me as your very own. I do not have a spirit of slavery (bondage) any longer, but I freely have received the Spirit of adoption, of which I cry, Abba, Father! Thank you, Lord, for removing the marks of slavery from my body, soul, and spirit. I love you, Lord. I am a child of the Most High God. In Jesus' name, Amen.*

---

*Adapted by permission from Kanaan Bedieninge, *Prayers of Renunciation* (Cape Town, South Africa: np., nd.), 199–203.

RENOUNCING HINDUISM

Dear heavenly Father, in the name of Jesus Christ, I confess my involvement in the deception and false doctrine of Hinduism. I admit that idolatry is an abomination in your sight and ask you to forgive my family and me for our involvement in the sin of idolatry.

- *I renounce the following Hindu scriptures as false, ungodly, and contrary to God's Word:*

    1. Upanishads (*based on the Vedas:* concentrated on philosophy and doctrines concerning reincarnation)
    2. Vedas (*Rig Veda:* songs of praise in honor of gods)
    3. Puranas (*ancient myths*)
    4. Bhagavad Gita (*songs of Hindu gods*)
    5. Sama Veda (*verses from Rig Veda,* used during rituals and sacrifices)
    6. Yajur Veda (*instructions for rituals related to sacrifices*)
    7. Atharva Veda (*magical formulas and verses for healing the sick and winning wars*)
    8. Brahmanas (*additional prescriptions concerning sacrifices and rituals*)
    9. Law Codes (*governing Hindu communities*)

10. Epic Tales

   a. Mahabharata (*taken from the* Bhagavad-Gita)

   b. Ramayana (*tale of the hero/god Rama*)

Lord, forgive me for attending and performing ungodly sacrifices or rituals. The sacrifices you require are a broken spirit and a contrite heart. This is the sacrifice I offer you right now, Lord. Father God, I present my body as a living sacrifice, holy, and acceptable to you.

- *I reject the false, wicked gods of Hinduism. I turn my back on them and break all curses assigned to me:*

1. Brahman *(creator-god)*
2. Vishnu *(sustaining god)*
3. Krishmi *(Vishnu incarnate)*
4. Shakti *(mother goddess; represents the kundalini serpent linked to the spinal column)*
5. Ganesh *(elephant god)*
6. Rama *(Vishnu incarnate)*
7. Kali *(another evil form of Shakti)*
8. Shiva/Sivan *(destroyer god)*
9. Surya *(sun god)*
10. *Any others*

- *I renounce the following teachings of Hinduism, along with any other philosophies or doctrines:*

1. Hinduism as a philosophy and confession of faith
2. Hinduism as a path of mystical insights
3. Reincarnation as the basis for eternal salvation (*nirvana*); "I cut loose from the wheel of rebirth" (*samsara*)
4. The law of karma (*determining destiny on earth*)
5. All sequences of Chakras or positions of the Lotus flower or Whirling Wheel (*a.k.a. the Wheel of Life*); "I cut loose from this wheel having been connected to the spinal column at several points"

6. The seven centers within the ethereal sphere outside of the physical, as well as any functions of these; i.e., use of psychic powers

7. The secret doctrines related to yoga and meditation and any cosmic scriptures

8. The Aryian Tribes in which Hinduism has its roots, as well as all their songs of praise and rituals to their gods (*Rig Veda*); *"I cut loose from the idea that the color of the skin determines a person's value. I renounce pride of thinking myself better than the untouchables."*

9. The three broad streams representing the wheel of rebirth; i.e.,
   a. philosophy of knowledge
   b. acts of religious observation
   c. commitment

- *I renounce reincarnation and manifestation. I turn my back on Hindu gods and walk away from ungodly altars. I sever unholy soul-ties with Hindu priests, any Hindu hermit and yogi, and confess this religion to be a lie and a deception.*

- *I renounce animal or human sacrifices related to Shavivism. Cleanse my hands of bloodshed. Forgive me for burns and wounds I inflicted upon myself to please the gods.*

- *I renounce the following roots of Hinduism:*

1. ascetism
2. meditation
3. physical breathing techniques
4. astral projection

- *I renounce Brahman (supreme god, rules the world with the help of lesser gods). I take back all territory from demonic spirits and his strongmen and close all doors to them.*

- *I renounce and break any cure by means of auras, the pendulum, bells, or the so-called "gong."*

- *I declare the following to be unbiblical and untrue:*
  - *The belief that all men are frozen energy*
  - *Having one's aura tested by means of the oscilloscope*
  - *The Chakra Wheel of color and light determining one's aura*

- *I renounce the Chakra Wheel and break its power over me:*
  - *Red* (earth chakra): *genetic coding, instincts*
  - *Orange* (moon chakra): *sex drive, fertility*
  - *Yellow* (sun chakra): *personal power*
  - *Green: heart center of astral light*
  - *Blue: controlling time*
  - *Violet: the arts, music, poetry, dance, drama, literature, sciences*
  - *White: center through which soul leaves body in astral projection*

- *I renounce the following teachings of Hinduism:*
  - *That the ego of man is transcendent and immanent, having no beginning or end, no birth and no death. That yoga is the synthesis of the physical and the metaphysical. Any form of mysticism, the occult, and sorcery*
  - *All the phases of yoga; i.e., controlling the body and subconscious, controlling the subconscious and blood circulation, mastering of any natural forces, mastering of black arts and sorcery*
  - *Any form of Silva Method, TM, yoga, mantras, and breathing techniques, mind control, self-hypnosis, rebirthing, hypnosis, ESP, spiritual activities, clairvoyance, visualization and meditation, and astral projection*

- *I also renounce Shakti and Shiva, whose union is said to awaken the kundalini force. I now separate and isolate Shaktim, Shiva, and the kundalini serpent and command them to leave me right now. I chase away their gatekeepers, tear up all their commission papers, and cancel all their instructions.*

  Spirits of darkness, I have all authority over you in the name of Jesus Christ. I bind and gag the spirit of perversion with the kundalini serpent attached, the spirit of witchcraft with the false doctrines attached, the spirit of antichrist with the false gods attached, and I command you to be quiet and powerless. All devils in these strongholds leave. Leave my mind, spine, organs, and body. I cast you off and out of me now in Jesus' name. (Keep repeating with authority until you sense breakthrough.)

Strongmen: get out of me. I forbid and reject your deception and lies. Loose me now. Loose my home, my possessions, and my family. Be gone!

Heavenly Father, please forgive me for giving the kundalini force control over my body by practicing yoga positions. I take up the sword of the Holy Spirit and allow that sword to sever my family and myself from this force. Father, I close these doors and seal them with the blood of Jesus.

Today I make an irreversible and binding decision to submit my spirit, soul, and body to the lordship of your kingdom—the kingdom of truth that is in Jesus Christ of Nazareth. Amen.*

---

*Adapted from Kanaan Bedieninge, *Prayers of Renunciation* (Panorama, Cape Town, South Africa: np., nd.), 89–110.

RENOUNCING THE MORMON CHURCH

Dear heavenly Father, I come to you in the name of Jesus Christ. I admit that I was involved in false teachings and ask for your forgiveness. Thank you that the blood cleanses and sanctifies me and the Word sets me free.

- *I renounce all faith in the* Book of Mormon, *compiled by Joseph Smith based on a meeting with the angel Moroni. I admit that I have sinned by adding this to the Word of God.*

- *I renounce all faith that the* Book of Mormon *is the verification and witness of the Bible. I sever and break free from all of Joseph Smith's false teachings.*

- *I renounce the two prince spirits that rule over the Mormon Church, namely, Moroni and Manasseh. I cut myself loose from these two demons in the name of Jesus.*

- *I renounce the teachings that:*
  - *God has a body of flesh and is thus limited to one place at a specific time.*
  - *Jesus' work of reconciliation is not for the salvation of souls but to save earth from death.*
  - *Jesus died only for Adam's sin.*

- *Our sins can only be washed away through baptism.*
- *The Holy Spirit is limited to only one place at a time.*
- *The Holy Spirit is the purest and most refined of all substances, a godly liquid.*
- *Every person is a god over his spiritual subordinates.*

- *I renounce the teaching that the fall of man has no effect on mankind and that every person will pay only for his own sin.*

- *I renounce the lie that the living may be baptized for the salvation of the dead. I confess that baptism is a testimony of my having been saved and not a requirement for salvation.*

- *I renounce the teachings that:*
  - *There is a highest heaven where the most exemplary believers shall live and reign over other believers in the same relationship that God the Father has with us.*
  - *There is a second earth-heaven where backslidden believers, those who did not accept God and those who did not abide by the law, shall live.*
  - *There is a place prepared (perdition) only for Satan, his fallen angels, and those who committed unforgivable sins.*

- *I renounce the principle of bigamy/polygamy and the implication that the number of wives a man has indicates levels of spirituality.*

- *I renounce the teaching that no woman can obtain heavenly splendor without her husband, likewise can no man obtain it without having at least one wife.*

- *I renounce the two principal councils that form the Mormon Church, namely Aaron's Priesthood and the Order of Melchizedek. I acknowledge that God's Word teaches that every believer is a priest and a king unto God.*

In the name of Jesus, I address the spirit of antichrist, the spirit of lies, and the spirit of error. I fasten you powerless. All devils in the stronghold of lies, antichrist, and error must leave now. I break your bonds, strip you of all strength, defeat your strategy, and command you loose me now. Get off my head and out of my mind, off my shoulders, out of my belly, be gone from my home and possessions. (Wait for a sense of breakthrough.) *Now, strongmen, I command you three to leave now and never return. I sever myself forever from the Mormon Church.*

- I confess that God the Father, the Son, and the Holy Spirit are *one,* although they function as separate personalities.

- I confess that the blood of Jesus Christ cleanses me from *all* sin—His sacrifice was perfect and complete!

- I confess that there is a *hell* where Satan, his fallen angels, and those who did not accept Jesus Christ will stay for eternity.

- I confess that there is a heaven where saved souls shall live until God has created the new earth and the new Jerusalem. Amen.*

---

*Adapted by permission from Kanaan Bedieninge, *Prayers of Renunciation* (Cape Town, South Africa: np., nd.), 87.

RENOUNCING THE WATCHTOWER (JEHOVAH'S WITNESSES)

Dear heavenly Father, I come in the name of Jesus Christ to thank you for convicting me of this false teaching. Forgive me for believing lies; I receive your forgiveness through the blood of Jesus. Now empower me as I make renunciation of a false religion.

- *I renounce the false teaching that only one person, namely Mr. [Charles Taze] Russell, can interpret the Bible, and I renounce every interpretation made by him.*

- *I renounce the doctrines that:*
  - *Jesus Christ is not part of the Trinity.*
  - *God created Jesus first.*
  - *Michael, the archangel, is the only begotten Son of God.*
  - *Michael, born from Mary, is the firstborn Son of God.*
  - *the Holy Spirit is not a person but an active force used by God to ensure that His will be done.*

- *the concept of the Trinity comes from Satan.*

- *I renounce the teachings of Judge [Joseph Franklin] Rutherford that:*
  - *there is no hell.*
  - *man consists only of a soul (ignoring 1 Thessalonians 5:23).*
  - *when I die, the soul becomes inactive and dead and thus can't go to hell—I don't exist anymore.*
  - *at the resurrection there will be a second chance.*

- *I renounce Jehovah's Witnesses teachings that:*
  - *Jesus is a god but not God, and the denial of His perfect mediatorship.*
  - *Jesus' life was not laid down for sin or judgment but to give me a second chance (trial of life).*
  - *it was not necessary that Jesus shed His blood for sin.*
  - *His suffering and death on the cross is irrelevant, while the fact that He was totally destroyed as a human being remains relevant.*

- *I renounce the teachings that:*
  - *only 144,000 believers will experience the blessing of heaven while the rest of the believers will have eternal life on earth if they prove themselves loyal through good works, faith, and loyal service.*
  - *man did not lose heaven because of sin but only paradise on earth.*

- *I renounce the teaching that God's judgment will last for a thousand years and is meant only as a period of probation for the living.*

- *I renounce the interpretation that Christ came in 1874, ascended to heaven in 1914, and that we now live in the thousand years of peace.*

- *I renounce the policy that as a new Watchtower member I must become a worker. I lay down this yoke of slavery in the name of Jesus.*

- *I renounce the belief that only the Jehovah's Witnesses are correct and that all other churches are as Babylon—under the control of Satan.*

- *I renounce the curse, expressed by [Charles Taze] Russell, that if I read the Bible and disregard the Studies in the Scriptures, I will be in darkness within two years.*

- *I sever myself from every teaching of Russell and break every curse over my spirit, soul (mind, will, and emotions), and body.*

- *I admit that Jehovah's Witnesses use the Scriptures out of context and distort them to their own destruction.*

By the authority I have in Jesus' name, I bind the spirit of witchcraft, the spirit of antichrist, and the spirit of lies, and command everything in the house-hold of these strongmen to loose me now. Every devil under these strongmen will leave now. I refuse and reject you! Leave now. (Progress once you feel a breakthrough.) *Now, strongmen of witchcraft, antichrist, and lies, I cut your cords and command you to leave and never return to me again.*

In the name of Jesus Christ, my Lord:

- I confess you are God as well as the *only way to the Father.*
- I confess you physically (bodily) were resurrected from the grave, and I renounce the lie that your body dissolved into gasses or is kept in a monument.
- I confess there will be a day on which every person will stand before God to be judged.
- I confess that:
  - Jesus became a *curse* to free me from the law of sin and death.
  - no one can go to the Father unless he accepts Jesus as Savior.

- I confess that I need to be born again to obtain eternal life.
- I confess that Jesus paid the full price on the cross for my:
  - transgressions—with His blood
  - sickness—by His stripes I am healed
  - iniquity—He was bruised for mine.

- I confess that God the Father, the Son, and Holy Spirit are one, although they function as separate personalities.
- I confess I have eternal life and am saved by grace, through faith and not by works—it is the gift of God.
- I confess that:

- there is a heaven and a hell, and that God will create a new earth and new Jerusalem for the righteous.
- the unrighteous that reject Christ shall suffer in hell forever.

Heavenly Father, cleanse my (conscious, subconscious, and unconscious) mind from all lies. I receive fresh revelation from the Spirit that will lead me into truth. Cleanse my spirit, soul, and body from any and all defilement. Thank you for your Word and for the blood of Jesus! Amen.*

---

*Adapted by permission from Kanaan Bedieninge, *Prayers of Renunciation* (Cape Town, South Africa: np, nd.), 5–10.

RENOUNCING SCIENTOLOGY

Dear heavenly Father, thank you for the revelation about the cult Scientology. Forgive me for believing lies. I receive your forgiveness of sins.

I reject and renounce, in the name of Jesus Christ of Nazareth, the following doctrines of the Church of Scientology:

1. *That man came to earth from outer space, and that man consists of four parts:*

   - *Thetan* ("THAY-ten"), the immortal spirit who can reincarnate
   - *a physical body*
   - *an analytical mind*
   - *an unconscious mind* (and that Thetan is in total control of the complete person, capable of generating tremendous power).

2. *That Thetan is responsible for the creation of the universe. That through time Thetan became so caught up in his own creation that his true greatness was forgotten, and that now it is only through Scientology's teaching that Thetan can again become conscious of his own potential.*

3. *That Thetan enters man's physical body through conception.*

4. *That man has an unconscious mind, which through shock, bruises, and pain*

can cause the analytical mind to become dysfunctional. That the unconscious mind then takes over and records the incident as an engram, *which in later life manifests as neurosis or psychological disorders.*

5. *The antichrist doctrine that when Thetan enters the body, all these engrams, contained during all the millennia of evolution, are received at birth.*

6. *That life is founded on the principle of survival.*

- *I reject and renounce the doctrine that a person's intellectual abilities and knowledge of himself are improved by Scientology.*
- *I reject and renounce the healing of sickness through* dianetics, *the modern science of spiritual health (do-it-yourself manual).*
- *I reject and renounce the Scientologist objective to become a* Clear. *(To have an IQ of at least 135, the highest creative vitality, deepest relaxation, and renewed memory.)*
- *I reject the seven grades of attaining* Clear *through progressive courses. I turn away from all these levels and break their power over me.*
- *I also reject and renounce the grades known as* Operating Thetan.
  - *I cut all soul-ties with all my advisors or counselors with the sword of the Holy Spirit, and I reject and renounce every session designed to overcome all sensitive inner parts of my life.*
  - *If my counselor used it to measure my stress levels, I reject and renounce the use of the E meter (Electro psycho meter).*
  - *I reject and renounce the theory that man is fundamentally good and that the cause of all his problems lies in past experience.*
  - *I reject the theory that only through Scientology can every man's problem be solved.*
  - *I reject and renounce the belief that salvation comes only though the paid sessions I had with my Scientology advisor.*
  - *I cut all unholy soul-ties or assigned familiar spirits with L. Ron Hubbard, founder of Scientology. I declare myself to belong to Jesus Christ, God the Father, and the Holy Spirit, spirit, soul, and body.*
  - *I reject and renounce ungodly baptisms, weddings, funeral rituals, and every other ritual and belief of which I am not aware. I declare a*

divorce from Scientology and destroy all rings, jewelry, and mantels, as well as all ungodly levels, ranks, and grades I attained.

I bind and gag the spirit of error, seducing spirits, and the spirit of antichrist, and every demon associated with Scientology. I command all demons in their stronghold to leave. Get out now. You have no strength in the house—your master is gone. I break all curses of insanity, false covenants, double-mindedness, and confusion. Every evil spirit, get away! (Wait for the breakthrough.) *Now I command the threefold strongmen to be loosed from me and never return.*

Thank you, Jesus, you've set me free. Amen! Amen!*

---

*Adapted by permission from Kanaan Bedieninge, *Prayers of Renunciation* (Cape Town, South Africa: np., nd.), 74–77.

RENOUNCING THE OCCULT AND NEW AGE PRACTICES

Father, my eyes have been opened to the power of the occult and New Age. This is sin against you. Please forgive me for my ignorance and for the associations of darkness I made while in the occult/New Age. Thank you for cleansing me of all sin. Amen.

I renounce involvement with the New Age movement. I acknowledge that rebellion is as witchcraft and an abomination in the eyes of God.

I renounce mass initiation through hypnosis, visualization, autosuggestion, hypnotherapy, and controlled imagery, which end in demon control.

I renounce all psychological therapies, meditations, bio-referral, positive confessions, hypnosis, holistic medicines, self-improvement methods, and success or motivational techniques.

I renounce all prosperity psychology, mind-psychology, willpower enlistment, metaphysics, and all forms of self-discovery (e.g., yoga).

I renounce all New Age healing techniques falling under the description of Alternate Healing, the source of which is satanic; these are abominations in God's sight. I reclaim all ground given to evil spirits through my participation in:

- acupuncture
- aired (Hindu art of healing and prolonging life)
- art (posters, idols, etc.)
- astral projection/astral flight
- astrology
- auras
- automatic writing
- bioenergetics
- biofeedback
- biorhythm
- black magic/white magic
- brain/mind development
- cabbala (mystic Judaism)
- centering
- chakras
- channeling
- chanting
- Christ's experience/out-of-body experience
- chromo therapy
- consciousness-expanding techniques
- contumacy (card reading)
- crystal ball
- crystals
- dianetics
- divining (or water dowsing)
- dowsing
- dream therapy
- *Dungeons & Dragons*
- electro-magnetic healing
- Feldenkrais method (awareness through movement; dangerous if spiritualized)
- fortune-telling
- gestalt awareness
- Gnosticism

- hypnosis
- I Ching
- imagery
- iridology (diagnosing through the reading of the eye's iris)
- kinesiology (unblocking energy meridians)
- kroning
- levitation
- macrobiotics
- martial arts
- massage (Reiki—radiance technique using universal "ki" energy)
- meditation
- metaphysics (contacting "God" with the mind instead of the spirit)
- near-death experience
- New Age herbalism
- numerology
- paganism
- palmistry (cheiromancy, cheiromography)
- parapsychology
- pendulum
- plant communication
- polarity therapy
- psychic abortion
- psycho cybernetics
- psychic surgery
- pyramid power
- rebirthing (breathing technique to cleanse human aura, to unleash psychic powers, and expand consciousness)
- runes (symbols believed to have magical significance)
- séance
- self-actualization
- self-healing
- self-hypnosis
- shamanism

- silva method (mind control, out-of-body projection, plus esoteric sciences)
- sorcery
- spiritism
- tantric sex
- tarot
- transactional analysis
- Transcendental Meditation (TM)
- triangle groups (groups of three: visualization and meditation, ushering in the New Age kingdom)
- Vedanta (classic monistic Hinduism)
- visualization
- water witching
- Wicca
- witchcraft
- yoga
- zen

I renounce, reject, and deny the power of the occult symbols of the New Age. I confess having worn, used as talisman, cast, meditated upon, or focused on as sources of power and/or used in rituals:

- all-seeing eye
- blazing star
- Centaur
- centering symbol (progressively smaller circles within a larger circle)
- circle
- circle divided into two
- circle divided into four
- crystal
- diamond
- dragon/serpents
- Egyptian ankh
- enneagram
- hexagram (Star of David)

- horned moon
- Italian horn
- lotus
- mermaid
- moon
- morning star
- Pegasus
- pentagram
- rainbow
- rays of light (to represent the seven rays)
- scarab
- 666
- sun
- swastika
- triangle
- unicorn
- wheel
- yin yang
- zodiac signs

I praise you, Lord, that I am free from the oppression of all New Age and occult powers as your Word says, "Ye shall know the truth, and the truth shall make you free" (John 8:32 ASV). In Jesus' name, Amen.*

---

*Adapted by permission from Kanaan Bedieninge, *Prayers of Renunciation* (Cape Town, South Africa: np., nd.), 145–71.

RENOUNCING ISLAM

Dear heavenly Father, I believe that Jesus Christ of Nazareth was born from the seed of woman (Genesis 3:15). That He was conceived by the power of the Holy Spirit and born from the Virgin Mary. I believe that God established His covenant with Isaac, Abraham's legitimate son, and not with Ishmael, the son of his bondswoman, it being an everlasting covenant (Galatians 3:16; Genesis 17:1–2). I believe that a Child (Jesus Christ) was born unto us; the rulership is upon His shoulders, and His name is Wonderful, Counselor, Mighty God, Everlasting Father, Prince of Peace (Isaiah 9:6 NKJV).

I believe that Jesus Christ is the only begotten Son of God and that whoever believes in Him shall not perish but have everlasting life (John 3:16; 1 John 4:10). Jesus Christ of Nazareth is the only Way, the whole Truth, and the eternal Life, and no one can come to the Father except through Him (John 14:6).

I believe that Jesus Christ died for my sins on the cross of Golgotha and that nobody else died in His place. The blood of Jesus Christ, the Son of God, cleanses me from all sin (1 John 1:7).

I believe that the Bible is the only inspired Word of God given for doctrine, for reproof, for correction, and instruction in righteousness

(2 Timothy 3:14–16). The Word of God shall never pass away or be replaced by any other book or word; the Word of God will stand forever, even though earth and heaven shall pass away (Matthew 5:18; 24:35; Isaiah 40:8; 2 Timothy 3:16). I believe that the Word of God was inspired by the Holy Spirit and not by the angel Gabriel (1 Peter 1:25; 2 Peter 1:21). I declare that the Gabriel who appeared to Muhammad was a counterfeit of Satan.

I believe in the triune God, and baptism in the name of the Father and the Son and the Holy Spirit (Matthew 28:19). God gave us His Holy Spirit [Greek *parakletos*], "the Comforter," and not "paracletas" [Arabic, "manhood"]. Jesus Christ is the same yesterday, today, and forever (John 1:1; Heb. 13:8).

I believe that Judas Iscariot betrayed Jesus Christ for thirty pieces of silver. Afterward he committed suicide by hanging himself; he did not die in Christ's place on the cross (Matthew 27:5; Acts 1:18–19). I believe that Jesus Christ himself died on the cross; no substitute was crucified in His place.

Father, I come to you in the name of your Son, Jesus Christ, and I repent for believing Islam to be the only and true religion.

I command the spirit of error, spirit of lies, spirit of fear, spirit of antichrist, spirit of witchcraft, and spirit of bondage to be bound and defeated.

I renounce the following teachings of Islam, that:

- *Christianity is false.*
- *Islam came into place because of Christianity's corruption.*
- *Converts to Christ are traitors to Islam, deserving of death.*
- *All Christians are blasphemers and have been deceived.*
- *The Qur'an is superior to the Bible.*
- *The Bible has been altered by translations and is no longer reliable as God's true Word.*
- *God had to send another true word (the Qur'an) to replace the unreliable Bible.*

- *Muhammad was the greatest and final prophet of God. I renounce the lie that Jesus Christ was only one of many other prophets.*
- *God sent Jesus Christ to establish Christianity, but that it became so corrupt that God sent Muhammad to establish Islam, and that Islam is God's final revelation.*
- *Jesus Christ is not the only Way to God.*
- *Jesus Christ is not the Son of God, and that God could not have had a physical son without having had sex with Mary.*
- *Jesus Christ didn't die for our sins on Golgatha's cross but that Judas Iscariot took on His likeness and died in His place as punishment for having betrayed Jesus.*
- *God is not the triune God; i.e., Father, Son, and Holy Spirit.*
- *Abraham had to sacrifice Ishmael instead of Isaac (Genesis 22:2, 9 proves the contrary).*
- *Mecca is a holy city by Muhammad's declaration.*
- *The Ka'aba (in Mecca) containing the black stone is a holy place (the black stone within it being a holy altar to Allah).*
- *Women are mere dogs, banned from mosque services. Women are on earth merely for the sexual pleasure of men.*
- *The Qur'an is the infallible, never-altered word of God, every word being the truth as revealed to Muhammad by the angel Gabriel.*
- *Repetition of Qur'an passages brings grace even without an understanding of the words.*

(*For Counselors:* The Qur'an does not state that the Bible has been altered. On the contrary, it states that a person who does not obey the Torah and the Bible amounts to nothing. The Qur'an contains several references to the Torah, Zabur [Old Testament], Psalms, and Injil [New Testament]. At the time of the Qur'an's first writing, the Bible's authenticity was never questioned—that deception came later. The Bible's entirety was on clay tablets and parchment scrolls more than half a millennium before Islam. [Some such ancient transcripts can be found in the London Museum and in the Vatican.])

I renounce blood sacrifices I have carried out, or in which I have partaken, and sever by the blood of Jesus any curses or bondages established in the spiritual realm by these rituals.

I renounce Jihad, the Holy War, through which it is an honor to kill or be killed for Allah.

I renounce the "Hadith," the record of Muhammad's life, and the standards he set for every Muslim.

I renounce the "Sunna," the example set by Muhammad, according to which every Muslim must live.

I renounce the ninety-nine names of Islam's God, to be repeated over and over, as well as the rosary used therein (with a name for every bead).

I renounce prayers to Allah facing toward Mecca, any prescriptions regarding the number of requisite times to prostrate, and all confessions of faith, ritual, and praise.

I renounce the hidden imam (or "Mahdi") whose coming is still awaited. I renounce any spokesman (Mujtahids) of this hidden imam. In the name of Jesus I sever soul-ties with them, as well as with any mullah or ayatollah.

I reject and renounce all Islamic holy days, along with their bondages and rituals.

I renounce the five pillars on which Islam is based:

1. *The Confession of Faith* (Shahada): *"There is no god but Allah, and Muhammad is the prophet of God."*
2. *Prayer* (Salat): *five times daily*
3. *Fasting* (Ramadan)
4. *Zakat (*alms*): 2.5% of income to be given to the poor.*
5. *Pilgrimage* (Hajj) *to Mecca at least once in a lifetime.*

I renounce the Cave of Hira and the Mountain of Light, where Muhammad received his so-called revelations from Gabriel. In the name of Jesus, I sever my family and myself from these false revelations.

I cut free from the false Islamic Calendar and from "Lailatul-Qadr" (the day on which Muhammad received the revelation).

I reject and renounce Allah, the moon god of Babylon (one of the 364 tribal gods of the Quarish tribe of Arabia).

I sever my family and myself from every group and faction of Islam. I cut soul-ties with teachers, imams, gurus, in the name of Jesus.

I once and for all renounce everything related to Islam. In the name of Jesus Christ of Nazareth, I take back what is mine and tear up every contract with demonic strongholds of darkness.

Thank you, heavenly Father, that Jesus, your Son, has set me free. I confess Jesus Christ to be Lord of my life. I have received redemption from my sin by His coming in the flesh, His blood, and His victory of resurrection. Amen.*

---

*Adapted by permission from Kanaan Bedieninge, *Prayers of Renunciation* (Cape Town, South Africa: np., nd.), 111–24.

RENOUNCING MARTIAL ARTS

- *I renounce the Asian arts of combat or self-defense (such as aikido, karate, judo, or tae kwon do) based on heathen deities and practiced as sports. I cancel all oaths and covenants to darkness with martial arts.*

- *I renounce two roots of karate, namely, the Chinese Martial Arts (including Kung Fu) and the Okinawese Martial Arts.*

- *I renounce Bhodidharma (Indian Zen Buddhist).*

- *I renounce any link with the Shaolin-Temple, from where karate originated and developed.*

- *I renounce Buddha as well as any form of worship or honor to him. I confess it as the sin of idolatry.*

- *I renounce the teachings of Zen (Find "God" in you. Find "Enlightenment" from within) and every Khatha (exercises) used as an aid for meditation.*

- *I renounce every discipline of the mind that seeks to make it my master.*

- *I renounce the teachings of Taoism, including that supernatural energy gives life to everything and maintains that life.*

- *I renounce "Ki" energy as well as "Kiai" I shouted to activate a better result in technique.*

- *I renounce Funakoshi ("father" of karate), who developed karate so that Zen can practically become a manner of life.*

- *I renounce the doctrine of karate on "the way of the empty mind" through the exercise of the body and mind, to obtain a new level of consciousness.*

- *I renounce every form of meditation:*
  - *mukoso (pay attention to the different positions, e.g., Lotus)*
  - *meditation through exercising sessions ("Moving Zen")*
  - *meditation through the repetition of basic karate principles.*

- *I renounce the purpose of karate:*
  - *the construction of better inner character*
  - *the removal of egocentricity*
  - *the discipline of the mind and body*
  - *meditation ("Moving Zen")*
  - *for the student to overcome himself, empty himself of his own ego, and develop a Zen-way of thinking.*

- *I renounce my faith in karate as one of the many ways that leads to life, and I renounce accepting it that way through earnest dedication.*

- *I renounce Khatha, every kick, and every war cry I used to summon demons to use their power. I confess it as sin and lay it down in the name of Jesus.*

- *I renounce special weapons (including Chaka-sticks) that I used, and I lay them down in the name of Jesus.*

- *I renounce pride and self-exaltation that worked through me, as well as belief in invincibility.*

- *I renounce spirits of self-destruction, destruction, murder, and death, in the name of Jesus.*

- *I sever the ungodly soul-tie between my master (Sensei _____) and me. I break any control he has over my mind in the name of Jesus.*

- *I destroy physically and spiritually all warring ranks that I received (belts; also any special awards/honoree titles).*

Spirit of pride, spirit of death, spirit of witchcraft, in the name of Jesus Christ, I bind your power. Devils under the strongmen, I command you to loose my family, my home, my possessions, and me. Leave immediately. (Wait for sense of relief.)

Strongmen of pride, death, and witchcraft, you're next. Out! Forever, and never return. Be gone!

Father, Jesus Christ is the way, the truth, and the life, and no one goes to you, except through Him (John 14:6). I freely bow down before you and my Lord and Savior. Thank you for cleansing me of all sin. Amen.*

---

*Adapted by permission from Kanaan Bedieninge, *Prayers of Renunciation* (Cape Town, South Africa: np., nd.), 51–54.

RENOUNCING UNBIBLICAL PRACTICES OF ROMAN CATHOLICISM

Note: Unbiblical or *extra-biblical?* There's a big difference between the two. Air-conditioned churches are extra-biblical (not mentioned in the Scriptures), but they're not unbiblical (contrary to what is clearly mentioned in the Scriptures). The following are not merely *extra-biblical;* they are plainly *unbiblical.* This is what a pastor friend said, having come out of Roman Catholicism:

> I personally know many Catholics that are saved, and they do not participate in unbiblical Catholic practices. I know that full revelation about Catholicism didn't come until after my salvation. When I first received Christ, it was like a blindfold came off, but as I renounced my involvement in certain unbiblical Catholic activities, I received understanding and revelation and then I had to

clean house myself. I think it's a two-step or even multi-step process. The blindfold comes off to accept Christ, and then the scales drop off as the sanctification process begins.
—Pastor Rene de la Cruz, Senior Pastor of Living Springs Community Church, Hesperia, California

---

I renounce the unbiblical sacrament of the baptism of children and the belief that baptism is one of the seven channels of grace through which I can hope to be saved.

I renounce the unbiblical belief that through baptism I have been cleansed of all my original sin, and that in so doing I have become a child of God and so have received eternal life.

I renounce the unbiblical belief that I have become born-again through the act of infant baptism. I also renounce my membership to the Roman Catholic institution and my loyalty to the law of the Roman Catholic Church.

I renounce my unbiblical loyalty to the Vatican and the yoke of bondage that was placed upon me through the Roman Catholic Church.

I renounce the unbiblical sacrament of confession to the priest and all acts committed in obedience to instructions that he gave me in order to earn my forgiveness, as well as the belief that it is not grace but works that saves me. I cut myself loose from the roots of this practice, namely, the worship of Ba'al, sun god in Babylon.

I renounce the unbiblical church structure—pope, cardinals, bishops, monks, nuns—and every statue, candle, holy water, and religious garb used.

I renounce the unbiblical use of the communion known as "Sacrament of the Holy Eucharist."

I renounce the unbiblical faith that the wafer becomes the body, the blood, and divinity of Christ and that I am to worship it as God himself.

I renounce the unbiblical roots of this practice rooted in Ba'al worship in Babylon. (Later Osiris, the sun god in Egypt, was worshiped in this manner;

the priest blessed round, unleavened-bread cakes that supernaturally changed into the flesh of their god.)

I renounce the unbiblical belief that the priest has so much power as to be able to remove Jesus from heaven and crucify Him again during the mass.

I renounce the unbiblical inscription on the wafer, I.H.S. *(In Egypt, three gods: Isis, Horus, Seb.)*

I renounce unbiblical bowing in front of and worshiping the wafer, as if it were God.

I renounce the unbiblical law, established by the Council of Trent, that a death penalty is upon those who do not believe that the communion wafer is God-incarnate. I cut myself loose from this curse in the name of Jesus. I confess that this communion element (the bread) is memorial and symbolic.

I renounce the unbiblical belief that during communion I was consuming the Creator of the Universe. I renounce the false teaching that in this way I received Jesus.

I renounce the unbiblical belief in the continual sacrifice of Jesus on the cross during communion, and I confess that He was sacrificed once for all as a perfect and complete sacrifice.

I confess that I had, by so doing, made Jesus a liar, and I ask for forgiveness.

I renounce the unbiblical sacrament of confirmation teaching hereby that I have received the baptism of the Holy Spirit.

I renounce the saint's name I unbiblically chose/was given at confirmation.

I renounce my membership to this church and break any other unbiblical oaths of loyalty.

I renounce Trent's unbiblical policy that cursed is anyone who confesses to have assurance of salvation. I break that curse in Jesus' name.

I renounce the unbiblical belief in the existence of a place called purgatory, where the soul is kept in suffering before it returns to heaven. I confess that I believed the lie that I could pay money to redeem anyone from purgatory. I ask forgiveness in Jesus' name. I confess prayer for the dead as sin.

*I renounce unbiblical faith in Mary (she was originally called Semiramis and later Isis and Venus). I renounce every prayer I addressed to her (*Note: This is not Mary of the Bible*).*

I confess as sin the unbiblical repetitive use of words, prayers to Holy Saints, kneeling in front of statues, the lighting of candles, the Sign of the Cross, with or without holy water, the sprinkling of holy water, and genuflecting in front of the altar.

I renounce the unbiblical appointment of a dead saint over me as my guardian (Hebrews 9:27). I cut myself loose in Jesus' name. I confess that there is only one mediator and that His name is Jesus Christ of Nazareth. I confess that He is the only way *to the Father (John 14:6).*

I renounce the unbiblical belief that the pope has the keys to life and death. I confess that these belong to Jesus Christ alone.

I renounce the unbiblical belief that the pope is the infallible head of God's kingdom on earth.

I renounce the unbiblical belief that Peter is the rock on which the Church is built. I confess faith in Jesus Christ, and Christ himself is the Rock.

I renounce the two unbiblical pillars on which the Church rests: that is apostolic succession *(starting with Peter) and* temporal power *(that the pope has authority over the kings on the earth).*

I renounce the unbiblical worship of women (Semiramis, "Mary") that wants to establish Satan's order on earth (Babylonian pattern).

I reject all unbiblical and *ungodly burdens/yokes placed upon me, not by God but by Satan.*

I renounce every unbiblical prayer I've prayed in the name of the rosary.

I renounce the unbiblical belief that when a priest blesses the rosary, each bead carries with it an indulgence (the remission of the temporal punishment that must be suffered for sins, either on earth or in purgatory).

I renounce the unbiblical belief that identifying with Mary's joy and suffering on earth can bring me closer to the Trinity or to her.

I renounce the way in which the following "mysteries" are used in conjunction with the unbiblical praying of the rosary.

- *I renounce the unbiblical belief in Mary's omniscience—that she can hear prayer anytime, from anyone, anywhere on earth.*
- *I renounce the unbiblical doctrine of the "immaculate conception"—that Mary is divine and had no human father.*
- *I renounce the unbiblical references to Mary as "co-redemptrix" (co-redeemer). Christ alone is the Redeemer.*
- *I renounce all unbiblical worship or honor that Mary has received through the Stations of the Cross.*
- *I reject all unbiblical worship of Mother Mary and her unbiblical identification with the Godhead.*
- *I renounce any loyalty or ties that I have with the unbiblical Queen of Heaven. I recognize only the authority and position of the Holy Trinity: God the Father, God the Son, and God the Holy Spirit.*

I renounce as unbiblical "giving up things" for Lent to win the Lord's favor through works.

I renounce the unbiblical belief that unbaptized babies go to "limbo" until enough prayer has been made for them.

I renounce every unbiblical novena ever made.

I confess that through my faith in Jesus Christ I have full assurance of salvation (1 John 5:11–13). I confess that the elements of communion are only symbolic of the body and blood of Jesus Christ. Thank you, Lord, that you now set me free. Thank you that the blood of Jesus cleanses me now. Thank you that the Sword of the Spirit now cuts me free from unbiblical practices of the Roman Catholic Church. I praise your name for the truth that sets me free. Amen.*

*Adapted by permission from Kanaan Bedieninge, *Prayers of Renunciation* (Cape Town, South Africa: np, nd.), 15–23.

RENOUNCING BUDDHISM

Dear heavenly Father, your Word says that we shall not turn to idols, nor make any molded images or gods (Leviticus 19:4). Neither shall we bow down to them or serve them, for you are a jealous God, visiting the iniquities of the fathers upon the children, to the third and the fourth generations of those who hate you (Exodus 20:4–5).

Your Word says that molded images are a falsehood, having no breath in them; they are futile works of error and a mockery in your sight (Jeremiah 10:14–15). Cursed is the man who trusts in man and makes flesh his strength, whose heart departs from you (17:5).

Father, in the name of Jesus I now ask you to forgive me, as well as my family, for our involvement in Buddhism, an idolatrous religion worshiping man above the Creator God, by whom we have been created.

I now renounce Siddhartha Gautama Buddha, *founder of Buddhism. I sever all unholy soul-ties with him, and any other Buddha coming after him, in the name of Jesus.*

I renounce both branches of Buddhism, as well as any other movements within Buddhism:

1. *Theravada* (little vehicle)
2. *Mahayana* (great vehicle)

I claim back the territory Satan has taken from me, and I tear up any contracts with Buddhism and Satan. I bind, rebuke, and loose the spirit of antichrist from my life. I renounce Buddhism as a vessel for carrying man across the world's oceans of suffering to a position of complete bliss and salvation. In the name of Jesus I leave this Buddhist vessel in the spirit world, turn my back on it, and walk away from it.

I renounce the following Buddhist doctrines and ask forgiveness for having believed in them. I bind all religious spirits, lying spirits, and false doctrines in the name of Jesus:

- *any doctrine related to the three baskets* (Tripitaka)
- *the* Vinaya Pitaka *(prescribed rules and regulations for the monastic orders and disciplines)*
- *the* Sutra Dharma Pitaka *(Buddha's doctrines, his life story, theories about the self and rebirth/reincarnation, the "three jewels," and the "precepts")*
- *the* Abhirdharma Pitaka *(dealing with the advanced doctrines and philosophies)*
- *the* Dhammpada *or "path of nature" (the oldest Buddhist text contains the "Four Noble Truths," the "Eightfold Path," and other teachings about morality and self-discipline)*
- *reincarnation (the heart of Buddhism)*
- *intense meditation*
- *not believing in a god (worship of images and idols; also worship of man)*
- *salvation as complete escape from the cycle of rebirth*
- *salvation as only possible by strict adherence to the "Noble Eightfold Path"*
- *meditation (to be balanced within oneself, exercising mind-control and abstinence from sensual experience)*

I renounce the "Eightfold Path," a compulsory set of rules in order to reach a state of Nirvana (salvation):

1. *The right way of thinking/believing*
2. *The right way of speaking*
3. *The right actions/deeds/emotions*
4. *The right way of concentration/meditation*

5. *The right means of living*
6. *The right effort*
7. *The right view of ecstasy/salvation*
8. *The right solutions*

I admit that I cannot achieve salvation by obeying rules and regulations—Jesus Christ of Nazareth is my only salvation. Good works cannot save me; only the grace of Jesus and the perfect price He has paid for me on the cross of Golgotha (Acts 4:12).

I renounce the Dhammapada *(path of nature) by which I strived to work out my salvation (Nirvana).*

I renounce the "Four Noble Truths" and other Buddhist doctrines teaching self-morality and self-discipline in order to reach Nirvana:

1. *To reach Nirvana, one must be willing to suffer, because all mortality is characterized by suffering.*
2. *To reach Nirvana, one must discover the true origin of suffering. Having discovered that, one must resist it (suffering originates in the impulses and desires of the self). Before Nirvana, all inner impulses and desires have to be killed by prescribed means, compulsory self-disciplines, exercises, chanting, and meditation.*
3. *Putting an end to all impulses and desires. By terminating all urges and desires, one puts an end to all suffering.*
4. *Following the way to abstinence from impulses and desires. (One can only achieve this by applying the "Four Noble Truths" and pursuing the "Eightfold Path," rules and regulations prescribed by Buddha.)*

I renounce any rules, meditations, chants, self-disciplines, and exercises in order to achieve salvation. The Word of God teaches that works cannot save me; salvation is by grace alone, for if it was by works, there would be no grace (Romans 11:6).

In the name of Jesus I sever any soul-tie with any priests or Lamas. I take back my territory and tear up any contract with Satan and Buddhism, in the

*name of Jesus. I renounce the worship or admiration of any image of
Buddha; e.g.,*

- *the largest one, in Daibutsi, Japan—a bronze cast*
- *Maitreya: the "laughing Buddha," giver of prosperity and wealth*
- *Amitabha: rules over the "virginal land" or western paradise on the other
  side of China's western mountains; also controls the vessel of salvation sail-
  ing over the sea of suffering/sadness on its way to paradise.*
- *at any pagodas or dagobas/wats built in honor of any Buddha, containing
  so-called "sacred" items; e.g., gold and a roof inlaid with diamonds.*

*I renounce any ambition to become like Buddha, i.e., to quench all impulses
and desires by pursuing a medium way between total carnality and living the
life of a hermit. I renounce the ambition to become an arhat, a being that has
reached a state of perfection. I also renounce the ambition to become a bodhi-
sattva, a being who has reached perfection (Nirvana) but has laid it down
because of a compassion for the suffering of his fellowmen.*

*I also renounce and ask forgiveness for my involvement in the "Wheel of
Dharma."*

*I renounce the "eye of wisdom" between the eyes of Buddha. (Counselor: close
and seal off the third eye.)*

Father, in the name of Jesus I ask you to sever the connection
between my spirit and my soul and to close and seal my third eye
with the precious blood of Jesus. (A Buddhist believes Nirvana [sal-
vation] is achieved when spirit and soul are merged. We believe salvation is by grace, not by works.)

I confess that your Word says to serve you joyfully, that your joy
is our strength, and that your joy will remain in us (John 15:11;
Nehemiah 8:10). Your Word is the joy and rejoicing of my heart
(Jeremiah 15:16). In your presence is fullness of joy; you have
clothed me with gladness, and the hope of the righteous will be
gladness (Proverbs 10:28; Psalm 16:11; 30:12). I also confess that
we learn obedience through suffering, and that Jesus suffered for

our sins on Calvary so that we could enter into the eternal joy of our Father.

I renounce the lies that change—through self-discipline, meditation, abstinence, and chanting—achieves karma (the unexplored law of cause and effect), which determines reincarnation; that every new life brings me closer to Nirvana; that only when this state has finally been achieved does karma cease.

I renounce the laws of abstinence in order to reach Nirvana:

- *No living creature may be injured intentionally.*
- *Nothing may be taken unless it has been given to you.*
- *Avoid sexual immorality.*
- *Avoid any lie or deception.*
- *Abstain from strong liquor or alcohol.*
- *Abstain from food on so-called holy days.*
- *Abstain from dancing/singing or pleasure.*
- *Abstain from personal jewelry or deodorant.*
- *Prohibition of luxurious beds.*
- *Prohibition of receiving or accepting any silver or gold.*

I renounce the false trinity of Buddhism, the so-called "three jewels" (triratna): *the Buddha, the Dharma (his doctrines), and the Sangha (order of priests). I renounce and sever from the roots of this false trinity in the name of Jesus.*

I renounce the "holy formula" to be repeated three times at any shrine or image of Buddha:

To the Buddha for refuge I go;
To the Dharma for refuge I go;
To the Sangha for refuge I go.

I renounce the so-called "holy of holies," the pagoda, and I ask forgiveness for having taken off my shoes as a token of being on "holy ground."

(Counselor: At the pagoda pilgrims can buy all kinds of golden objects to be brought as sacrifices to its statue of Buddha, such as leaves, flowers,

incense, lanterns, rosaries, bells, dolls, drums, combs, and buttons [some of which may have been kept].)

Father, I ask you to forgive my family and me for offering sacrifices to Buddha. I ask you to burn any such sacrifice in the spirit world with your consuming fire.

I ask forgiveness for having possessed an idol or ornament in the form of Buddha or the Laughing Buddha, which are false gods. I reject curses, yokes, or false covenants in my house and on my life. I declare that I am cleansed by the blood of Jesus Christ, my Lord and Savior.

I also ask your forgiveness for every time that we have struck the big bell to call the heavens and the earth as witnesses to our deeds of humility. I sever myself and my family from the earth and the heavenlies *[in this regard]* and ask that you destroy their witness against us with your consuming fire.

I renounce every one of these practices and turn my back on them, as well as the ritual of covering my face in my hands, bowing down, kneeling, and prostrating myself in front of him. I ask forgiveness for having chanted any of the liturgy or scriptures, the burning of incense and inner sacrifices, or staring at his image in an attitude of worship.

I ask forgiveness for any chants involving the rosary. I ask forgiveness for shaving my head as a Buddhist token. I hand back my priestly robes, beggar's bowl, and other such possessions. I ask you to destroy any spiritual "level" that I might have reached in the spirit world.

I renounce all rituals related to the initiation into the priestly office. I renounce the "Lotus Sutra Sakyamuni" (glorified Buddha of China). In the name of Jesus I sever any soul-tie with him.

I renounce any ambition to be a Buddha upon reaching the state of Nirvana. I declare that in everything I do, everything I own, and everything I say, I will have but one ambition: to be like my Lord and Master, Jesus Christ of Nazareth.

I renounce any form of meditation in honor of Buddha (i.e., CH'AN or ZEN). I turn my back on anything related to Buddhism and walk away from it in the name of Jesus.

Thank you, Father, that I can know you today as being merciful and forgiving, having removed my sins from me as far as the east is from the west, having forever set me free from the sin of idolatry and false Eastern religions. Thank you, Father, for your infinite mercy and love. All this I pray in the precious name of Jesus. Amen.*

---

*Adapted by permission from Kanaan Bedieninge, *Prayers of Renunciation* (Cape Town, South Africa: np., nd.), 132–43.

PRAYER FOR HEALING OF MEMORIES

Make this your own personal prayer.

Jesus, thank you for dying on the cross—not only for my sins, but also for my hurts and fears. You are the same yesterday, today, and forever, and your desire is that I be completely whole: spirit, soul, body, and mind. Lord, please walk back through every moment of my life, to heal every part. Go back three and four generations of my ancestors, to the first man, and remove all harmful generational iniquity.

Jesus, you knew all about me before I was born. Thank you for being there as my life began. If fear or trauma was transmitted to me in my mother's womb, dissolve it now for your kingdom's sake. You chose me before the foundation of the world, set apart to love and to bless you on this earth.

Lord, during my preschool years, fill every hurt, rejection, abandonment, or abuse I may have experienced. Take away my fears of darkness, of falling, of authority, or betrayal. Thank you, Jesus, for setting me free in these areas.

Lord, at school, there were times when I felt inadequate, not part of the "in crowd," and unattractive. I release to you all those sad and troubling memories. Heal my hurts and turn my pain into a heart of compassion for others. Help me to trust you to take the fears that entered during those years. I praise you for touching me and freeing me.

Jesus, thank you for my mother [or stepmother, grandmother, guardian, aunt, friend; if you didn't have the love of a mother, release your questions of why, your anger, or your disappointment, to the Lord right now]. Stand between my mom and me and let your unconditional love flow between us. Forgive me for any way I have failed, hurt, or rebelled against her; I forgive and release her from all hurt I may have experienced at her hand.

Lord, thank you for my father [or stepfather, grandfather, guardian, uncle, friend; if you didn't have the love of a father, release your questions of why, your anger, or your disappointment to the Lord right now]. Stand between my dad and me; I pray that divine unconditional love will mend any brokenness. Forgive me for when I dishonored, betrayed, or rebelled against him; I forgive and release him from all guilt and shame where he may have hurt, disappointed, or failed me.

I lift up my brothers and sisters to you. Where there were feelings of competition, jealousy, envy, or resentment, I allow your healing power to mend these hurts and any broken relationships. I forgive them for any hurt I experienced. I speak a blessing to each one now. [Name each sibling.] Bring reconciliation through me.

Thank you, Lord, for your presence in my teenage years. As I grew older I had to deal with new emotions. As each painful memory is brought to mind, wipe the pain from my mind and heal me. During those times I tried ungodly things that were dangerous. [Acknowledge what you did and ask for His healing and restoration.] Thank you for your hand of protection when I was so foolish. Take away any humiliation, embarrassment, guilt, shame, or fear, both for what I did and for what others did to me. [If you were teased or *ridiculed or otherwise abused, bring this before Him.]* You are a God who redeems . . . thank you.

After leaving home, I had frustrations and hurts. *[Maybe you wanted to go to college and weren't able to; perhaps you weren't able to enter the profession you dreamed of, and disappointment has stopped your passion. Share anything that applies to you.]* Jesus, heal every disappointment and every wound.

Thank you for your help as I entered marriage. *[Whether it was a beautiful new beginning or a dream dashed.]* Jesus, take away the pain of disappointment or false expectations. I pray that you will stand between *[my mate]* and me and heal every hurt, every lost opportunity for growth in love and forgiveness. I forgive *[my mate]* for misunderstanding me, for times of isolation and verbal wounding, and for pain of all kinds, real or imagined. Jesus, thank you for mending broken relationships and strength to honor and keep our vows. I choose to release all bitterness and regret.

Thank you for my children. Forgive me where I have failed as a parent. Where I punished unwisely or was too possessive with my love, where I spoke critically or angrily, I pray you will heal any hurt I have caused. I too forgive *[my children]* for any hurts intentional or unintentional. Starting now, I pray our relationship may be better than ever.

Lord, thank you for your presence during times of sorrow. Thank you for taking my hand to walk through the valley with me. I praise you for lifting the burden. I receive your joy and your peace.

Old things are past, and I look forward to new beginnings. In the name of Jesus I make this declaration. Amen.*

---

*Adapted by permission from Kanaan Bedieninge, *Prayers of Renunciation* (Cape Town, South Africa: np., nd.), 82–86.

ENDNOTES

CHAPTER 1

1. See article from Thomas Brooks, at *www.bible.org*.
2. All scriptural emphasis has been added.
3. Rebecca Greenwood, *Breaking the Bonds of Evil* (Grand Rapids: Revell, 2006), 13.
4. Chris Hayward, "Deliver Us From Deliverance Ministry" in *Ministries Today* (Jan./Feb. 2006): 51–53.

CHAPTER 2

1. Adapted from R. H. McCready in *Best Modern Illustrations* (New York: Harper and Brothers, 1935), 315.
2. Sam Levenson, *You Don't Have to Be in Who's Who to Know What's What*, in Charles R. Swindoll, *The Tale of the Tardy Oxcart* (Nashville: W, 1998), 145.
3. Adapted from Craig Brian Larson, *Illustrations for Preaching and Teaching: From* LEADERSHIP *Journal* (Grand Rapids: Baker, 1999), 37.
4. For a broad look at how to break free from victimization, see my book *Beyond the Lie* at *www.prayerbookstore.com*.
5. To learn how, purchase our book *Spiritual Housecleaning: Protect Your Home and Family From Spiritual Pollution* at *www.prayerbookstore.com*.

CHAPTER 3

1. Adapted from J. Oswald Sanders, *A Spiritual Clinic*, in Charles Swindoll, *The Tale of the Tardy Oxcart* (Nashville: W, 1998), 198.
2. In ibid., 53.
3. John Killinger, *To My People With Love*, in Craig Brian Larson, *Illustrations for Preaching and Teaching* (Grand Rapids: Baker, 1993), 35.
4. Source unknown.
5. G. B. F. Hallock in *Best Modern Illustrations* (New York: Harper & Brothers, 1935), 326.

CHAPTER 4

1. *Webster's Seventh New Collegiate Dictionary* (Springfield, MA: G. & C. Merriam Co., 1970), 1037.
2. Source unknown.
3. Carl F. Keil and Franz J. Delitzsch, *Biblical Commentary on the Old Testament;* see at *www.e-sword.net.*

CHAPTER 5

1. Mark Twain, in Burton Stevenson, *The Home Book of Proverbs, Maxims, and Familiar Phrases* (San Francisco: W. Clement Stone, 1984), 344.
2. J. Oswald Sanders, *For Believers Only,* in Charles R. Swindoll, *The Tale of the Tardy Oxcart* (Nashville: W, 1998), 155.
3. Chuck Pierce, in Doris Wagner, *How to Minister Freedom* (Ventura, CA: Regal, 2005), 42.
4. *Webster's Seventh New Collegiate Dictionary* (Springfield, MA: G & C Merriam Co., 1970), 1032.
5. Ibid., 519.
6. Paul E. Holdcraft, *Snappy Stories That Preachers Tell* (New York: Abingdon-Cokesbury, 1932), 343.
7. For more insight on this subject, see *Beyond the Lie* (*www.prayerbookstore.com*).

CHAPTER 6

1. Alice Smith, *Beyond the Lie* (Minneapolis: Bethany House, 2006), 39–40.
2. From *Strong's Greek Concordance;* see at *www.e-sword.net.*
3. Ibid.
4. From Finis Jennings Dake, *Dake's Annotated Reference Bible* (Lawrenceville, GA: Dake Bible Sales, 1963), 193.
5. *http://truthinconviction.us/comments.php?id=121_0_1_0_C*
6. *www.courthousechurch.org/sermons/ephesians2.1–10.html*
7. *www.crimelibrary.com/notorious_murders/women/tucker/2.html*
8. *www.crimelibrary.com/notorious_murders/women/tucker/1.html*
9. *www.courthousechurch.org/sermons/ephesians2.1–10.html*
10. Adapted from *http://truthinconviction.us/comments.php?id=121_0_1_0_C.*
11. Op. cit.

CHAPTER 7

1. *Webster's Seventh Collegiate Dictionary* (Springfield, MA: G. & C. Merriam Co., 1970).
2. Ibid.
3. Ibid.

4. For example, see
   www.punahou.edu/acad/sanders/geometrypages/GP03Polygons.html;
   www.newton.dep.anl.gov/newton/askasci/1993/eng/ENG1.HTM;
   www.math.com/school/subject3/lessons/S3U3L4GL.html;
   www.promotega.org/uga05004/FCP_Glossary.html;
   www.madsci.org/posts/archives/2002–01/1009992903.Eg.r.html.

CHAPTER 9

1. Charles R. Swindoll, *The Tale of the Tardy Oxcart* (Nashville: W, 1998), 218.
2. From Paul Holdcraft, *Cyclopedia of Bible Illustrations,* from *Sermons in a Nutshell* (New York: Abingdon-Cokesbury, 1957), 24. Adapted into contemporary language.
3. Alice Smith, *Beyond the Lie* (Minneapolis: Bethany House, 2006), 111.

RECOMMENDED READING

Neil Anderson, *Victory Over the Darkness*, Ventura, CA: Regal, 1990

John Bevere, *The Devil's Door*, Lake Mary, FL: Charisma House, 1996

Mary Ann Collins, *Unmasking Catholicism*, New York: Universe, Inc., 2003

Kimberly Daniels, *Clean House, Strong House*, Lake Mary, FL: 2003

Francis Frangipane, *This Day We Fight*, Grand Rapids: Chosen, 2005

Rebecca Greenwood, *Breaking the Bonds of Evil*, Grand Rapids: Revell, 2006

Jack Harris, *Freemasonry*, New Kensington, PA.: Whitaker House, 1983

Chris Hayward, *God's Cleansing Stream*, Ventura, CA: Regal, 2004

Peter Horrobin, *Healing Through Deliverance* (Vols. 1 & 2), Grand Rapids: Chosen, 2003

Cindy Jacobs, *Deliver Us From Evil*, Ventura, CA: Regal, 2001

Vito Rallo, *Breaking Generational Curses and Pulling Down Strongholds*, St. Louis: Free Indeed Ministries, 1999

Don Richardson, *Secrets of the Koran*, Ventura, CA: Regal, 2003

John Sandford and Mark Sandford, *Deliverance and Inner Healing*, Grand Rapids: Chosen, 1992

William J. Schnoebellen and James R. Spencer, *Mormonism's Temple of Doom*, Boise: Through the Maze, 1987

Alice Smith, *Beyond the Lie*, Minneapolis: Bethany House, 2006

———, *Beyond the Veil*, Ventura, CA: Regal, 1997

———, *40 Days Beyond the Veil*, Ventura, CA: Regal, 2003

Alice and Eddie Smith, *Spiritual Housecleaning*, Ventura, CA: Regal, 2003

Eddie Smith, *Breaking the Enemy's Grip*, Minneapolis: Bethany House, 2004

William and Janet Sudduth, *Deliverance Training Manual*, Pensacola, FL: Righteous Acts Ministry, Inc., 2000

Doris Wagner, *How to Minister Freedom*, Ventura, CA: Regal, 2005

MINISTRY RESOURCES

(1) DAVID KYLE FOSTER

(Homosexuality, Lesbianism, and Sexual Dysfunctions)
Mastering Life Ministries
P.O. Box 351149
Jacksonville, FL 32235
904-220-7474
www.masteringlife.org

(2) PETER HORROBIN

(Healing for Rejection, Loss, and Inner Pain)
2310 Leonard Drive
Seffner, FL 33584
813-657-6147
813-657-4983 (FAX)
www.usa@ellelministries.org

(3) SHERILL PISCOPO

Evangel Christian Churches
28491 Utica Rd.
Roseville, MI 48066
www.evangel-churches.com

(4) CHRIS HAYWARD

(Inner Healing, Abuse, Christian Growth)
Cleansing Stream Ministries
P.O. Box 7076
Van Nuys, CA 91409–7076
www.cleansingstream.org

(5) KIMBERLY DANIELS

(Gangs, Deliverance, Drugs, Sexual Problems)
Spoken Word Ministries
9197 Camshire Dr.
Jacksonville, FL 32244–7425
www.kimberlydaniels.com

(6) *http://christianbest.com/xian_wom.html*

A comprehensive list of Christian organizations that help with various issues: homelessness, abuse, personal growth, single parenting, etc.

(7) *www.counselcareconnection.org*

(Anger Management)

(8) GERI MCGHEE

(Deliverance, Soul-Ties, Strongholds)
Abiding Life Ministries
15684 C.R. 434A
Lindale, TX 75771
www.abidinglifeministries.org

(9) JEFF VANVONDEREN

(Spiritual Abuse)
P.O. Box 7481
Capistrano Beach, CA 92624
Voice: 949-677-8354;
E-mail: *jeff@spiritualabuse.com*
www.innervention.com
www.spiritualabuse.com/dox/contact.htm

(10) VITO AND PAT RALLO

(Depression, Sicknesses, Deliverance)
Free Indeed Ministries
9266 Estate Cove Circle
Riverview, FL 33569–3103
813-626-0497
www.freeindeedministries.org

(11) BIBLICAL DELIVERANCE MINISTRIES

P.O. Box 301109
Albany 0752
Auckland, New Zealand
E-mail: *support@christianwarfare.co.nz*
www.christianwarfare.co.nz

(12) DALE SIDES

(Strongholds, Healing of the Mind, Abuse, Deliverance)
Liberating Ministries for Christ International
P.O. Box 38
Bedford, VA 24523
540–586–5813
www.lmci.org/

(13) SELWYN STEVENS

(Spiritual Deception; Freemasonry; Mormonism; Watchtower; Christadel-
phianism; Spiritualism; New Age [including alternative/occult healing
therapies]; Islam, Baha'i, etc.)
Jubilee Resources International
P.O. Box 36–044
Wellington 6330
New Zealand
www.jubilee-resources.com